TAROT
OF TALES

ACE OF COINS

ACE OF CUPS

ACE OF SWORDS

ACE OF WANDS

TAROT
OF TALES

THE LITTLE GUIDEBOOK

0 THE FOOL

VIII STRENGTH

XVIII THE MOON

MELINDA LEE HOLM

Illustrations by
ROHAN DANIEL EASON

CICO BOOKS
LONDON NEW YORK

Published in 2023 by CICO Books

An imprint of Ryland Peters & Small Ltd

20–21 Jockey's Fields   341 E 116th St

London, WC1R 4BW   New York, NY 10029

www.rylandpeters.com

10 9 8 7 6 5 4 3 2

Text © Melinda Lee Holm 2023

Design © CICO Books 2023

Illustrations © Rohan Daniel Eason 2023

A CIP catalog record for this book is available from the Library of Congress and the British Library.

ISBN: 978 1 80065 199 9

Printed in China

Commissioning editor: Kristine Pidkameny

In-house editor: Jenny Dye

Senior designer: Emily Breen

Art director: Sally Powell

Creative director: Leslie Harrington

Head of production: Patricia Harrington

Publishing manager: Penny Craig

CONTENTS

INTRODUCTION 6

The Language of Tarot 6

Your Story 8

Writing the Ending 9

THE BASICS 10

Preparing for Readings 10

Asking Questions 11

Reading Between the Lines 12

SPREADS 14

Narrowing Focus 14

Finding the Path 14

Navigating Influences 15

MAJOR ARCANA 16

MINOR ARCANA 62

Suit of Cups 64

Suit of Swords 92

Suit of Coins 120

Suit of Wands 148

Acknowledgments 176

FIVE OF SWORDS

INTRODUCTION

We tell ourselves stories to make sense of our lives. Whether individually in a journal, in pairs or small groups with trusted friends, or collectively in folk tales and myths, telling our stories reframes our experiences, allowing us to learn and grow from them and to see the present as a moment continually suspended between the past and the future. Sometimes the story we are living in can seem unclear or overly complicated. Tarot helps us to focus and clarify what is going on in our lives, to hear and tell the story we need in order to move forward, and it uses its own special language to do so.

THE LANGUAGE OF TAROT

When I first started reading tarot, I began by doing readings for myself, laying the cards out over and over to get familiar with their forms, colors, and symbols, and how they looked and felt together. I looked up the meaning of each card and considered it in the context of the name of the spread position, each card + position combo a little island of guidance. At the same time, I dove into studying the meaning of each card individually and how people have interpreted the card differently over the years as well as how the cards were grouped (suits, numbers, associations) and what commonalities these groups shared. As my knowledge increased, I pushed myself by setting down the books to see what I could understand on my own. Once I was confidently familiar with the stories and meaning of all 78 cards, I began to see new complexity emerge in the messages of my spreads, more nuance, even poetry. I gained fluency.

This is roughly the same process we go through to learn any language. We immerse ourselves through movies and music, learning simple songs to get the sounds into our minds and mouths. We cover the walls with posters of foods and other images labeled with the words of the language. We acquire vocabulary as we use the language, first in simple declaratives and then in questions, and finally nuanced expression. Little by little, we put down the dictionary and push ourselves to speak using the knowledge we've built. We practice and practice and take ourselves from clumsy to poetic.

Tarot is a language. Each of the cards can function as verbs, adjectives, nouns, as single words or whole paragraphs, expanding and contracting as needed. We ascribe meaning to different positions in spreads and lay out the cards to form narratives, arguments, comparisons, and inquiries. We see the guidance of the individual cards shift and grow when combined with other cards. The layers of text, imagery, and symbology embedded in tarot decks combine to bring us their unique expression of this language. There are only 78 cards that together can express all of human experience. In order to do that, they must each be able to hold many layers of meaning. You won't understand them all right away. In fact, it is good practice to hold the view that none of us will ever understand all of the ways tarot can speak to and about us and our lives. Languages constantly evolve to serve the time and place they are used in. Tarot is no different.

Like any language, periods of joy and frustration come as familiarity and then fluency are built. The reward for hard work and dedication is the ability to see the world in a new way, a way that can only be described using the language of tarot. Be patient with yourself as you expand your vocabulary and fluency. Converse with others who are further along in their studies. Seek out multiple voices. In time you too will develop your own unique way of speaking in this magickal language of tarot.

XIV TEMPERANCE

YOUR STORY

Tarot of Tales is written and designed to invite you into the world of your personal story. For each card, you will find a brief overview of the card and five possible card interpretations or meanings written in narrative form, parts of your story waiting to be linked together. Simply follow the spreads on pages 14–15 and string together the pieces of narrative that correspond to the positions to read the story of your chosen topic or situation. Our stories are complex. There is so much more going on around the main action—other characters having their own journeys, settings shifting and evolving—than can ever be told in one tale. Fortunately, you don't need to know everything all at once. One of the great gifts of tarot is that it can guide you to focus on specific aspects of your story that need your attention so you can spend your energy where it will be most beneficial.

You are the main character of your own story. There are many other characters in your story—supporting roles, background characters, and even villains. They all have their own stories too. What their motivations and intentions are may be interesting, but they do not have a direct impact on how you, the main character, work through issues as your story develops. In other words, *Tarot of Tales* is here for you to discover and explore you. What emerges will likely have an effect on how you interact with the other characters in your story, but you're the one we're all rooting for. This is your story.

SEVEN OF COINS

WRITING THE ENDING

So how does your story end? That is entirely up to you. The beauty of viewing your readings as chapters or paragraphs in a story is that you then get to imagine what you want to happen next and, with the guidance of your reading, begin to take steps to get there. We all come from somewhere, we're all going somewhere, and we all have our own set of tools and circumstances to work with and within. As you work with these cards and see all the different parts of your story unfolding, step outside yourself, observe yourself as you would the protagonist of your favorite book or movie, be proud of the ways you see yourself grow, and maintain a hopeful curiosity about how you will choose to end this story and begin another.

TWO OF SWORDS

EIGHT OF SWORDS

THE BASICS

The text and illustrations in *Tarot of Tales* draw on symbols from fables and folk tales. Just like in folk tales, going into the woods, meeting a queen, or journeying to the bottom of the sea are metaphors for experiences we may encounter in our own lives. For example, venturing into the woods is a common narrative symbol for facing fears, so there is an image of a bunny rabbit entering a dark forest on the card associated with facing fears, The Moon (see page 54). Read the stories of your tarot spreads as you would a fairy tale to find the guidance offered to you. To help you connect these passages more directly to your own life, there are keywords and phrases at the beginning of each card's entry. Since *Tarot of Tales* follows the format of a traditional 78-card tarot deck, you can also use your existing knowledge of tarot to inform your readings.

When you read your stories in the spreads of *Tarot of Tales*, there are going to be places where the segues seem a little odd or the story jumps from one setting to another. That's okay! With over two and half billion possible five-card readings, the text is not always going to fit together in a perfect flow of poetic language and logical transitions. This is where your imagination and intuition have their time to shine. Let the places in between exist as canvases for your own understanding. If you are notating your readings in a journal (which I highly recommend) you can leave a little room in between the cards to jot down your ideas on how you could get from point A to point B and what happens during that part of your journey.

PREPARING FOR READINGS

Before you begin to work with *Tarot of Tales*, take a moment to explore the world of the deck. Look over the cards and notice if you have any reactions to individual images, characters, or realms. Touch every card and shuffle the deck several times. This will welcome the deck into your life and act as an icebreaker in your relationship as partners in metaphysical exploration.

When you are ready to begin your reading, make sure you have a quiet place where you can focus. Remove distractions and clear the energy by burning herbs or incense, using a spray made for energy clearing, or ringing a bell you keep for this purpose. Have a journal and something to write with nearby. I like to light a candle to indicate that I am opening a connection with the universe and that this time and place is dedicated to exploring that connection through the tarot.

ASKING QUESTIONS

Possibly the single most important skill you can develop to get more out of your readings is the art of asking questions. Begin by deciding what area of life, topic, or situation you want to look into, then shuffle the cards while asking "What story do I need to hear about ___?" Keep your question open ended, especially when working with *Tarot of Tales*. Asking a yes/no question and receiving an answer in the form of a story might be fun as something you'd experience on a trip to Delphi to visit the oracle, but it's probably not going to be very clear or helpful here and now. Asking what story you need to hear allows the cards to answer you with all their wisdom and reminds you that there are many stories of any situation and that this one will be most helpful at this time.

For those pressing do-they-or-don't-they love interest questions, asking "What story do I need to hear about my relationship/dynamic with ___?" can be illuminating, but "What story do I need to know about my love life?" is even better. Looking at your love life (or work life or friendships) overall and then viewing a person or dynamic through that lens is not only more informative, it empowers you to take action based on the guidance you've received instead of waiting to react to someone else.

QUEEN OF CUPS

READING BETWEEN THE LINES

The cards don't always have the same feel in every reading or situation. What is easy or welcome for one person or context, may not be for the next. When working with the tarot, there are a few common ways to determine whether a particular card may present a bit more of a challenge or invite an alternative way of looking at it—reversals, proximity to other cards, and intuition.

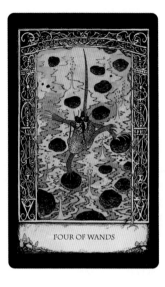

FOUR OF WANDS

When a card is upside down when it is turned over, we call that card "reversed." Some readers read the reversals and leave the card upside down, others don't and instead turn all cards right side up. Reversals can indicate that the energy of that card will be delayed, that it will be experienced more internally than externally, or will be experienced in a way that could be perceived as negative. Whether you read reversals and how you choose to interpret them is completely up to you. If you do choose to read reversals, decide on their indication in advance so you and your deck are speaking the same language.

There are cards that have meanings or stories that are inherently complementary to each other, while other cards conflict. Considering the cards in your readings as personalities existing in a room together and then determining whether there is anyone in that room who might get along exceptionally well (or not well), is a great way to see different feelings in the cards. This is the method I use along with the third method, intuition.

Sometimes a certain card in a reading will make me nervous for no obvious reason. Or a card that is generally considered difficult might feel light and joyful. This is my intuition guiding me to view that card in a different way than I normally might and it adds to the meaning and the guidance I get from my readings. Trusting your intuition to guide your readings in this way takes some practice. Take notes and stick with it.

With *Tarot of Tales*, there is another way to see nuance in the cards: the narrative. All of the stories you have read, heard, watched, and told throughout your life inform your reading of every new story you encounter, including the ones you will read with this deck. As you explore *Tarot of Tales*, notice how the narratives of your readings fit into your personal bank of tales. Are you afraid of water and keep ending up in the realm of the sea? Are your journeys unfolding in a way that reminds you of a character you've always had an affinity for? You are the expert on your own history and taste. Let your personal history combine with our collective human history of storytelling to bring deeper meaning to the fantastic journeys that await you in *Tarot of Tales*.

III THE EMPRESS

SPREADS

These spreads are designed to work with the text on pages 18–175, bringing your stories to life by linking different aspects of the cards according to their positions. Shuffle the cards, thinking of your question, until you feel they've really heard you. Then, you can either cut the deck into three piles, choose one, and pull your cards off the top, or you can spread the deck out in front of you with the cards face down and choose each card from anywhere in the deck. Either way, know how many cards you are drawing for your spread before you begin. Use these spreads on their own or as building blocks, linking them up to create more complex narrative structures.

Narrowing Focus

Sometimes, simplicity is best. A concise message can speak volumes to guide you or focus your thoughts around a topic or situation. This single card "spread" is excellent for daily pulls or for deep inquiry. Choose which of the card's entries you're going to read ahead of time or read them all and see which one resonates most.

Finding the Path

1   In the past…

2   At present…

3   On the horizon…

1   2   3

When you want to see the direction something is going in (and where it's come from), nothing beats a classic past/present/future spread. Place the cards from left to right. Need more information on the past, the present, or the future? Pull more than one card for that position, using "and" to connect the messages of the cards.

**Navigating
Influences**

1 In the past…

2 At present…

3 From above…

4 Deep within…

5 On the horizon…

3

1

2

5

4

Throughout our lives, influences impact how we perceive and navigate situations, some internal and some external. This spread lends insight into what may be pulling or pushing on you. Pay attention to how the passages in these cards make you feel and whether they seem logical or unexpected in the context of your question and story.

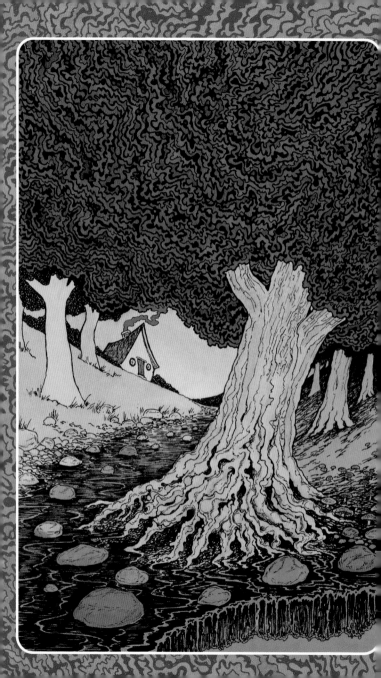

MAJOR ARCANA

The 22 cards of the Major Arcana represent archetypes found in stories throughout time and throughout the world. While our view of these characters may vary with time and culture, their core essences—the release of Death, the undeniable power of The Emperor, the deep reflection of The Moon—connect us in universal human experience.

0 THE FOOL

0 THE FOOL

Radical presence, trust, surrender to the moment, awareness, letting go of the past and accepting all possible futures, the joy of simply being

In the past…
you had a carefree attitude, never concerning yourself with plans for the future. You trusted that exactly enough would come to you at exactly the right time, freeing you to follow your bliss with a clear mind and heart.

At present…
your eyes are locked with the eyes of a performing dog, balanced on a ball on one foot and juggling yet exuding a tranquil bliss so complete that you wonder if she'll fall asleep. Your sense of time melts away. This moment is your whole world.

On the horizon…
colorful flags in a variety of sizes, shapes, and patterns dance in the breeze. No two are alike and yet they all seem to be celebrating the same thing. You feel yourself begin to sway along to their rhythm as you approach.

From above…
songs of birds combine with the rattle of tree branches in whistling wind to create a spontaneous improvised symphony. This music of nature beckons you to set down your work and dance to the rhythm of life.

Deep within…
a profound stillness keeps you grounded in the here and now. Everywhere you go, a sense of calm contentment follows. You feel free to play, not weighed down by guilt over this idle time, but instead buoyed by the happiness it brings.

I THE MAGICIAN

Manifestation, realization, self-actualization, the creation of one's own life, balance of the five classical elements, connection to the power of the universe

In the past…
the life you had was not right for you. You closed your eyes and imagined a new one, and your future world was born. The full Moon smiled down on your vision, the Earth offered her gifts, and your journey to bring it all to fruition began.

At present…
you are hard at work conjuring the life you desire from materials you have on hand. Everything around you is exactly what you need if you look at it with a rat's cunning eye. You point your wand at the shelves and let it lead the way.

On the horizon…
an eclectic group is gathered, some young, some old, all wise. You can feel their power from here. It feels familiar. You reach up to touch your talisman and take a step forward. Fireworks explode in celebration of your approach.

From above…
a fine, sparkling dust falls gently around you like a light snow. You hold your hand out to catch it, but it absorbs instantly into your skin the moment it touches you, sending a pulse of warmth through your body.

Deep within…
an alchemical process is taking place, combining all of your powers with those of the Earth and the universe. Your own personal magick is taking form. Others can sense it and begin to react to you differently.

I THE MAGICIAN

II THE HIGH PRIESTESS

II THE HIGH PRIESTESS

Devotion, ritual, sanctity, boundaries, caring for your temple, travel between worlds, introspection, fruition, reflection, veneration

In the past…
you often felt drained. To get the rest you needed, you created a little space with no distractions where only you and the divine were allowed to be. That space became your temple; those boundaries, permanent.

At present…
the temple glows as you light the candles on the altar one by one, reciting an incantation for each. Your bare feet are silent on the worn stone floor, your movements as smooth and fluid as a ghost.

On the horizon…
a stone structure stands on a hilltop, a statue of a goddess of the Moon guarding its door. A priestess emerges from the temple to light incense at the base of the statue. You feel you've been there before and know you will be again.

From above…
the full Moon smiles down on you, illuminating everything around you in its cool, reflected light. You smile back, gazing up through a perfectly clear sky and begin to arrange stones in a circle, defining a sacred space for your work.

Deep within…
your mind, there is no barrier between the Earthly and spirit realms. You move easily between the two, gathering wisdom and honoring those who carried it before you, always taking care to close the veil as you pass from one world to the other.

III THE EMPRESS

Gathering abundance, receiving by giving, love, beauty, fecundity, cultivation, acceptance, organic growth, relaxed elegance, generosity

In the past…
you spent long hours in your garden, planting, pruning, weeding, watering, never feeling fatigued or depleted. This experience instilled in you a trust in natural processes and in your own ability to grow what you need.

At present…
you survey the bounty of your garden with pride. Every day here is worthy of celebrating, so you dress elegantly to dig in the soil, the city mouse and country mouse all in one, caring for these plants that give so much in return.

On the horizon…
a rosy hue colors the sky and clouds to match the flower field below, infusing the landscape with a warmth and softness that relaxes your mind and opens your heart. You move ahead with confidence. This is your place.

From above…
a gentle fluttering of wings lifts your attention from your work. Dozens of butterflies in a rainbow of colors dance in the sunlight above your head. They are drawn to the beauty you've cultivated and the gracious love that helps it grow.

Deep within…
you know that any room you enter is your room, immediately filled with your love and generosity of spirit. You expect to be accepted, meeting everyone with an open heart, and your unguardedness and grace assure that you are.

III THE EMPRESS

IV THE EMPEROR

IV THE EMPEROR

Leadership, vision, direction, authority, seeing the big picture, long-term planning and execution, empire building, management, supervision, setting standards

In the past…
you stood to speak, tentatively at first, then, emboldened by the rapt attention of your peers, with conviction. The power of your words and the soundness of your logic made you the perfect candidate to step forward as leader.

At present…
you talk your team through your strategy. Everything is laid out on the table in detail. Success is not the goal, it is imperative. Everyone leans in close to hear the plan, holding complete trust in you and your eagle-eyed vision.

On the horizon…
heraldic flags bearing your coat of arms on tall poles billow in the wind. Beneath them, a line of troops, armor shining in the light, stands perfectly still, so still that at first you mistake them for statues. They await your command.

From above…
something pulls at the top of your head, straightening your spine into perfect posture. The posture makes you feel different, more powerful. You lift your chin and see your surroundings with new eyes.

Deep within…
your being, a fire blazes, threatening to consume you from within if it is not released. You try running, painting, writing, anything you can think of to slow its burn. But there is only one thing that will. You must step into your power.

V THE HIEROPHANT

Tradition, spiritual teaching, passing on sacred knowledge, learning, trust in process, dedication, faith, an established course of study, discipline, lineage of wisdom

In the past…
an important and beloved teacher gave you invaluable wisdom that changed your relationship with yourself and the divine. A library of all you learned stands proudly on a shelf of well-worn books and tucked away in your heart.

At present…
creatures gather at the foot of an ancient tree to hear the teachings of a storied elder. Predators and prey forget their usual roles, becoming students and keepers of sacred wisdom for now. You join them, honored to have the privilege.

On the horizon…
gnarled branches reach into the sky from a distant hilltop. Pilgrims pass you as you stand still on the trail, some offering you provisions, others deep in thought as they make their way to seek teachings from the oldest living being on Earth.

From above…
songs blow in on every breeze, your eye catches the same words over and over again on billboards and buildings. The messages can no longer be ignored. Follow the signs. You are being called to serve a greater role in the enlightenment of the world.

Deep within…
your spiritual ideals are rising to the top of your consciousness. They condense into mist, swirling around you, a protective aura. You pay more attention to your words and actions, aware of the weight they have and the responsibility to wield them wisely.

V THE HIEROPHANT

VI THE LOVERS

VI THE LOVERS

Balanced partnership, compatibility, mutual admiration, symbiosis, interdependence, the joy of sharing control, attraction of opposites

In the past...
a beautiful meditation garden took shape through work with a beloved partner. The result was much more exquisite than either of you could have accomplished alone. This shared sanctuary showed you your own strengths and the value of trusting others.

At present...
life buzzes all around you as bees pollinate the flowers of a lush garden. You watch one disappear into a blossom and emerge covered with a fine dusting of pollen and for a moment you think you see the petals close in a loving embrace.

On the horizon...
a dying stream of smoke barely drifts out of the chimney of a cottage on the hillside. Though you long to sit in the garden, you do your part to keep your home fire burning, turning back to the forest to gather wood.

From above...
a sound like laughter floats down to your ears. You look up and see birds dancing in the sunlight, chirping cheerfully to each other as they gather building materials for their nests, working together to create a place of beauty and a refuge.

Deep within...
your heart, there is space capable of infinite expansion, enough to fit the whole world. But for now, you breathe pink light into this space for only one person, doing your part to heal and strengthen your side of a partnership.

VII THE CHARIOT

Arrival of assistance, forward movement, recognizing and accepting help that is right for you, rising to the next level, separation of the self from the vehicle

In the past…
heavy rain turned the ground to thick mud. You trudged forward, your boots growing heavier and heavier with each step. Just when you thought you could not go on, a vehicle arrived. You pulled your feet from your boots and climbed inside.

At present…
you stand frozen on the sidewalk, unsure which way to turn. A carriage pulls up and the door swings open, velvet upholstery glowing in the afternoon light. It seems too easy, but somehow you know you must shake away your doubt and step inside.

On the horizon…
dust swirls in low clouds on the ground. A noise like thunder emanates from the dust, though there are no storm clouds in the sky. The first chariot emerges into view, the leader in a race, all headed toward you.

From above…
the flapping of heavy wings announces the arrival of a massive bird. You duck in fear to avoid its sharp talons, but the bird is too quick and gently picks you up and sets you in a plush basket hanging around its neck.

Deep within…
a struggle is raging. You fear that if you accept help with your work, it will no longer be your own, but you know you can't accomplish what you want to do alone. You put your hands on your heart for reassurance and prepare yourself to receive.

VII THE CHARIOT

VIII STRENGTH

VIII STRENGTH

Unseen power, confidence, knowledge of one's own gifts, personal gravity, a silent announcement, public presence, the art of persuasion

In the past…
you ran yourself ragged trying to be the person you thought you were supposed to be until you got too tired and gave up. With no energy for pretense, you discovered how powerful and unique your natural presence is.

At present…
your hammock sways in a light breeze, rustling the pages of your book and cooling your skin in the afternoon sunlight. Your mind is perfectly calm, your heart content, knowing you have nothing to prove and no one to impress.

On the horizon…
flashes of light twinkle above the ground, catching your eye. You squint your eyes and see a row of binoculars trained on you, their lenses catching the sun. You calmly wave hello and go back to living your life.

From above…
some sort of magnetic force pulls you up, lengthening and stretching you into your largest form. Your limbs tingle as waves of energy pulse through your body, powering you up to beam your light out to the world.

Deep within…
a ball of golden light is growing with each breath, filling your torso, then your limbs and head. Your skin starts to tingle and you know it won't be long before this light breaks free from your body and shines out into the world, a beacon of your power.

IX THE HERMIT

Seclusion, purpose, inquiry, study, synthesizing information, forming a thesis, lighting the way, transformation, emergence, being your own best companion, tranquility

In the past…
intellectual discussions made you nervous. You felt awkward and anxious working in a group of people you admired. Crestfallen, you retreated and found that ideas you could bring back to the group flowed easily. Alone time was essential to your work.

At present…
you inhale deeply and the scent of incense and old books fills your lungs. There is no sound but the crackling of the fire, keeping you warm as you dive deeper into your studies, forming your unique conception of your world.

On the horizon…
a dense and unfamiliar forest looms, yet you are not afraid. Instead, you feel pulled into the darkness. A light flickers in the window of a distant cottage illuminating a table piled high with scrolls and manuscripts.

From above…
calls to adventure beckon, but not to far-off lands. You yearn for an exploration of the mind, gathering knowledge and wisdom. There is something the world needs to know that only you can discover. You have a mission.

Deep within…
you know there is more to this life than meets the eye and you know what you must do to discover the secrets waiting to be revealed to you. You gather the books and supplies you will need and quietly detach from public life.

IX THE HERMIT

X THE WHEEL OF FORTUNE

X THE WHEEL OF FORTUNE

Patience, luck, trusting in the perfect timing of the universe, the right thing at the right time for the right reason, expansion, unexpected developments or delays

In the past...
you thought you had control over when big changes happened in your life, but you were proved wrong. Happily wrong. Delays led to unexpected adventures. Accelerations showed you how prepared you already were.

At present...
you wait impatiently for your turn to spin the wheel. Others in line laugh and chat amongst themselves, enjoying the chance for social connection. You overhear a conversation that sparks your interest and lose track of how long the line takes.

On the horizon...
a thick fog obscures your view of the terrain. Travelers pass you and disappear into the cloud, chatting excitedly about a carnival up ahead. You'd like to join the fun, but decide to sit and enjoy the scenery while you wait out the weather.

From above...
a gust of wind due to a sudden change in air pressure disorients you. Clouds gather above and you see figures in their forms—a bear, bird, lizard, and ant. Their faces seem to all turn toward you, offering assurance and protection.

Deep within...
you know that things may not be going how you'd like now, but that doesn't mean they won't turn out in your favor. You say a silent thank you to the universe for taking care of you and for the good fortune headed your way.

XI JUSTICE

Balance, equality, harmony, fairness, a need to reassess where and how energy is spent, course correction, resolution, working smarter not harder

In the past…
you threw yourself into your work, becoming consumed, working late nights and early mornings. At the end of a project, you were utterly exhausted and depleted, forced into rest. The downtime gave you the space to see the importance of pacing yourself.

At present…
raccoons take turns playing on a makeshift seesaw. A bear tries to join the fun, but is too heavy. The raccoons find a fair solution that allows everyone to be included, piling on top of each other to balance the weight of the bear.

On the horizon…
bright blue and pink plumes of smoke shoot up into the light of the setting sun. You watch the colors swirl together and wait for them to meld into one big purple cloud, but they stay separate, forming a pattern of perfect symmetry.

From above…
a chorus of voices sings a series of chords, the notes weaving together perfectly into complex harmonies, each taking a turn to rise, supported by the others. You begin to hum a tone, adding your single note to the chorus.

Deep within…
you feel a heaviness weighing down your spirit. Your efforts to ground yourself have worked too well. You think of a moment of excited joy to bring butterflies to your stomach, restoring your equilibrium.

XI JUSTICE

XII THE HANGED MAN

XII THE HANGED MAN

Shift in perspective, the path less traveled, embracing the unfamiliar, inspiration, elevation of the uncommon, taking time to see things differently

In the past…
you tripped over a stone on a walk through the forest and fell to the ground. From your new vantage point on the ground looking up, you saw a whole new forest, patterns in the branches, a cornucopia of mosses and mushrooms.

At present…
a colony of bats sleeps away the day, hanging from the branches of a tree, their wings wrapped around their bodies. Except one. A single bat stands upright, wings outstretched, drinking in a view no other bat has ever seen.

On the horizon…
a perfect mirror image of the landscape is reflected in the sky above. The air between the tips of the trees of this world and the upside down world vibrates and shimmers. You wonder what you look like to someone standing in the world above.

From above…
a hand reaches down to tap you on the shoulder. It is you, happily hanging upside down from the branch of a tree. You beckon yourself to climb up and you oblige, taking your spot next to yourself on the branch, seeing the world anew.

Deep within…
your stomach churns. You try to be as still as possible to stop it, but stillness only makes it worse. As you move around, you find that the churning settles only when you are in a position you have never been in. You need the unfamiliar.

XIII DEATH

Release, rebirth, making room for new growth, acceptance of the body and its vulnerabilities, fearlessness, the cycle of life, letting go, celebrating life

In the past…
you mourned the passing of time, the loss of youth, the changing of the seasons. The sight of a delicate green shoot growing up through the ashes of a fire shifted your focus from mourning death to celebrating the resilience of life.

At present…
scorched land stretches out before you, charred remains of the landscape still smoking. A skeleton dances, not for the destruction but for the new life it promises. You join in the celebration, a raven cries out in camaraderie.

On the horizon…
dark smoke hangs in the air beneath the eerie orange glow of sunlight obscured by ash. Animals and birds crowd the space around you, refugees from the fire. You take a moment before continuing forward to the realm of death.

From above…
a raven swoops down to circle you, its caw growing more and more urgent. There is a message for you from the underworld. You open your arms to drop what you've been carrying and tilt your head up to listen.

Deep within…
your body, a hollow space grows. As it grows, debris from your past is cleared out. Old wounds, painful memories, and unfulfilled hopes all detach and fall down into the Earth to be transmuted, making room for growth.

XIII DEATH

XIV TEMPERANCE

XIV TEMPERANCE

Moderation, mindful focus, optimism, boundaries around time and energy, healing, stillness, prioritizing peace and wellness, reserve, acting with intention

In the past...
you felt pulled in too many directions, never having quite enough time or energy for any single pursuit. To reset, you pulled back from everything, then let your heart decide what deserved your attention and when.

At present...
serenity fills your being as you sit at the edge of a placid pond. You breathe deeply and take in the scenery, the perfect symmetry of the landscape and its reflection in the pond. A unicorn calmly gazes back, sensing your peaceful nature.

On the horizon...
the land lies perfectly flat, the trees still. There are no clouds in the sky. You shout into the distance and your voice echoes back as if bounced off an invisible wall. You inhale deeply and count as you exhale.

From above...
the scent of violets drifts down and envelops you. You inhale and feel imbued with quiet determination, stretching each of your limbs, first the left side, then the right, readying yourself to be the protector of your peace.

Deep within...
a connection with the Earth secures you to the ground, drawing your energy downward, while an equal and opposite connection with the sky pulls your energy upward, holding you in perfect suspension.

XV THE DEVIL

Determination, projection, assumptions, false standards, imagined rules and limitations, earthly concerns, potential, recognizing internalized oppression, breaking free

In the past…
your body felt heavy. Every step took great effort and you were perpetually exhausted. You sat down to rest and saw that your legs were bound by thick vines. You cut yourself free and pulled the vines out of the ground by the root.

At present…
a silhouette looms large on the wall. You stand frozen, transfixed by the power it has over you. The halo of light around it moves and the spell is broken. It is just a mouse in the beam of a flashlight once again.

On the horizon…
a formidable thicket of thorns rises, taller than a house, blocking the way ahead. Your heart sinks, then something catches your eye. Cutting tools are laid out in front of the thorn hedge. You prepare yourself for the work ahead of you.

From above…
a clap of thunder and crash of lightning announce the arrival of a terrible storm. Lifting your head to assess the danger, you see lightning strike a falling tree, destroying it before it lands on the house below.

Deep within…
a fear of loss consumes you. You cling to belongings and people. When one leaves, it becomes clear how much you were drained by the relationship and your worst nightmare becomes your greatest gift.

XV THE DEVIL

XVI THE TOWER

XVI THE TOWER

Destruction, collapse, breakdown of what seemed unbreakable, freedom, impermanence, unexpected changes, the chance to reset the rules

In the past…
you obediently followed tradition, accepting the rules and mores followed by your parents and their parents before them. A tragedy sent your world crashing down. When the dust settled, you found you had new freedom to live your own life.

At present…
the ground beneath your feet begins to shake as bricks fall from above. You run to find cover from the chaos and watch a tall tower you thought would stand forever crumbling. Your mind fills with images of what you can build with the fallen stones.

On the horizon…
a large tower looms over the village below. Narrow openings allow authorities to see out, but no one can see in, a perfect system of control. Dark clouds gather and a lightning bolt flashes, striking the tower and breaking its walls.

From above…
you feel eyes watching you, judging your every move, making sure you follow the rules. You long to be free from their prying eyes. A loud crash startles you and bricks begin to fall all around. A new world is possible.

Deep within…
a voice calls to you, directs you to behave in specific ways. The voice has sounded less like your own lately and you wonder where it came from and how you internalized its perspective. The first crack in the wall.

XVII THE STAR

Hope, nurturing, eternity, the lineage of life in the universe, promise, guiding light in the darkness, ancient unbroken chain of creation

In the past...
you sat alone at the edge of a forest in the dark, feeling lost. Clouds parted in the sky just in time for you to see a shooting star. You make a wish and lean back to find a deer, rabbit, and squirrel all sharing this moment with you.

At present...
animals gather to gaze up at the morning star, shining brightly in the emerging dawn. Predators and prey, territorial rivals, huddled in a moment of peaceful community, grateful for the promise of another day.

On the horizon...
the sun drops out of view, revealing a galaxy of stars twinkling in the night sky. One stands out, brighter than the others. As you look at it, its light grows in intensity and pulses, transmitting a message only for you.

From above...
the soft flap of leathery wings fills the silence as bats hunt insects in the golden glow of sunset. The sound reminds you of the interdependence of the world, each being with its own purpose, all caring for the continuation of life.

Deep within...
a light glows, your own personal lantern illuminating the way ahead. You feel calm, assured, cared for. A sense of purpose appears in the light, a need to bring this feeling to others, to nurture the wellbeing of those around you.

XVII THE STAR

XVIII THE MOON

XVIII THE MOON

Reflection, facing fears, journeys into the subconscious, resurfacing memories, stepping into unknown territory, collective consciousness

In the past…
you dove deep into a dark pool to find the root of your fear, pulled it up, and emerged freer and stronger. In the light, the fear was nothing much to look at and you wondered how it ever had such a hold on you.

At present…
you stand at the edge of a dark wood, hesitant to venture further. Shadows on the trees morph into menacing figures and your heartbeat quickens in fear, but you know you must continue on into this mysterious and unknown world.

On the horizon…
a placid lake reflects the full Moon in its perfect stillness beckoning you to jump in. Shapes across the lake seem to move, or is it a trick of the eye. You hesitate, then step forward to face the unknown.

From above…
plays of light and shadow catch your eye, but when you look up, there is nothing there. You have an eerie feeling that something is now hiding just out of your view. The phantom presence has your attention.

Deep within…
a profound stillness anchors you in your body. You sense there is more to your story, more to learn about who you truly are. You hold your head high, proud of who you are discovering, alone in the darkness.

XIX THE SUN

Clarity, truth, revelation, illumination, accepting reality, emergence, directing growth, cultivation, bravery to see and be seen, the known world

In the past…
you made your way through a thick fog, tripping over things until you were covered in bruises. When the sun came out and burned the fog away you saw these hazards for the small and avoidable inconvenience they really were.

At present…
a butterfly pulls itself from its cocoon into the sunlight, stretching its wings for the very first time, this new form on display for all to see. You are inspired and begin to wonder what cocoon you are emerging from.

On the horizon…
rocky hills rise out of a flat desert landscape. The terrain appears completely barren, but if you look long enough, signs of life are everywhere, tiny plants, snakes flicking their tails. The truth of the desert for anyone to see.

From above…
rays of sunshine beam down to warm your skin and the top of your head. You take in the radiance of this star, so close to Earth, and begin to think about the true nature of everything, including yourself.

Deep within…
clarity radiates from the center of your being out through your fingertips. You are aware of your bones, the tendons connecting them to your muscles, your blood vessels. You are no longer a mystery to yourself or anyone else.

XIX THE SUN

XX JUDGMENT

XX JUDGMENT

Excavation, evaluation, confrontation of the past, discovery, treasure hunt, supporting the future, healing old wounds, the gift of discernment

In the past…
while cleaning out a closet, you stumbled upon a trinket that stirred up strong emotions that needed to be set free. Digging further, you found gifts, evidence of loves past, some to cherish and some to let go.

At present…
a miniature trunk pops out of a hole in the ground. A rabbit's face emerges then retreats into the hole to continue clearing out the clutter. You feel a vicarious sense of catharsis that begins your own clearing process.

On the horizon…
plumes of dust shoot up from different places in the ground intermittently, in short bursts, like a release of pressure. The color of the dust varies and you wonder what causes it and what exactly is being pulled up to the surface.

From above…
a voice that sounds like yours sings praises of your future. You strain to hear the details, but can't quite make them out. To prepare for any eventuality, you set to work clearing out what you don't need from your house, heart, and head.

Deep within…
parts of you that have been solidified for many years are breaking apart, revealing their contents. Memories, emotions, experiences that made a big impact, some treasured, some you'd rather forget. This is your chance to sort them out.

XXI THE WORLD

End of an era, new beginning, a portal moment, the time in between, contraction, crossing a line in the sand, the next phase, leveling up

In the past...
there was a confusing time when it seemed like random things and people were being removed from your life. It didn't make sense until the dust settled and you found yourself living a new and improved version of your life.

At present...
the mouth of a massive cave gapes before you. Your lantern allows you to see just a few feet in front of you. You empty your pockets, taking only essentials as you step ahead into this portal to a whole new world.

On the horizon...
tall cliffs rise up from rolling hills. You check your map. You have followed it correctly, but this formation is not recorded. An opening appears in the cliff face. You pause to compose yourself before venturing into uncharted territory.

From above...
an energetic field descends upon you. It touches the top of your head and you start to buzz. You close your eyes and feel it pass down your whole body. When you open your eyes again, the world glows as if you are seeing in technicolor.

Deep within...
something has shifted. You see the world differently. There is something more you have to offer, a new way to live as an individual and a community member. You begin to use new language to bring this change out into the open.

XXI THE WORLD

MINOR ARCANA

The 56 cards of the Minor Arcana are divided into four suits.
Each suit contains Ace to Ten cards and four court cards,
and corresponds to one of the four classical elements.
In *Tarot of Tales*, these elements are translated into the
different realms of the world of the deck. The suit of Cups
represents elemental Water, realm of the sea. The suit of
Swords represents elemental Air, realm of the sky. The suit
of Coins represents the element of Earth, realm of the forest
and mountains. The suit of Wands represents elemental Fire,
realm of the desert and volcanoes.

ACE OF CUPS

ACE OF CUPS
Realm: The Sea

Divine love, emotional support, loving without fear, love independent of relationships, emotional certainty, open heart channel, personal relationship with the Divine

In the past…
you looked for love in others, not believing you could love yourself on your own. It was stressful and unpredictable. You waded into the sea to calm your nerves and felt your body awaken and fill with unconditional love.

At present…
a golden chalice gleams in the sunlight filtering through the sea. Corals have grown up around it, thriving in the warm glow. You too are drawn to the chalice, and you float comfortably in the water taking in its power.

On the horizon…
you see something sparkle through the seaweed, up in the shallows. A rainbow of color surrounds the sparkle, a thriving coral reef, and you have to look away for a moment to let your eyes adjust to the intensity of light and color.

From above…
a warm current reaches down to envelop you. As it flows around you, it washes away debris collected around your heart over decades and you feel your heart swell and expand into this new space the current has created.

Deep within…
your heart, a little piece of stardust glows, shining the love of the universe all through your body and out into the world. Others sense it. Simply being in your presence awakens the stardust in their hearts, and the cycle of love continues.

TWO OF CUPS
Realm: The Sea

New love, feeling a spark, connection, being open to meeting new people, optimistic vulnerability, offering the benefit of the doubt

In the past…
you regarded kind strangers with suspicion, always keeping a distance to protect yourself from getting hurt. But the distance itself started to hurt, so you let someone in and were rewarded with a pure and true love.

At present…
two fish entwine in a loving embrace, guarded by the tentacles of a protective jellyfish. You smile at them as you swim past and wonder what new love will grow in your own life and what or who will protect it.

On the horizon…
a pink glow pulses, sending waves of desire out into the open ocean. You feel their invitation drawing you closer and soothing your fear and defenses. Your feelings develop before you ever see what they are for.

From above…
sunlight warms the surface of the water, drawing you up into the most richly populated part of the ocean. All kinds of life surrounds you and you find yourself relaxing into the possibilities each potential interaction holds.

Deep within…
your being, the seeds of self-love you planted are growing and blossoming. Receptors are opening, inviting new bonds to form. You are ready for new love to grow and for old love to grow anew, looking forward with an open heart.

TWO OF CUPS

THREE OF CUPS

THREE OF CUPS
Realm: The Sea

Mutual support, trusted confidantes, celebration of friendship, intimate conversations, chosen family, shared experience, pooling resources

In the past…
you shied away from small gatherings, nervous you would have nothing to say or worse, say the wrong thing. An old friend coaxed you out of your shell and into the embrace of their group of trusted confidantes.

At present…
you gather with friends for a tea party, hosted on the back of a friendly sea turtle. The conversation flows easily and you revel in the love and trust you share. Everyone is dressed up to express, not impress.

On the horizon…
laughter bubbles up, sending pulses of joy rolling out all through the sea. You feel a smile spreading across your face and a warmth growing in your heart. Though you are alone for the moment, you are not lonely.

From above…
something is gently pulling on your hair. You run your hand across your head a few times, thinking it is the current, but when it doesn't stop you look up to see cheerful faces smiling down at you, inviting you to join their party.

Deep within…
a sense of pride grows in your heart as you think about the friends that have become your family and the family you've formed true friendships with. These bonds are so strong that you are never truly apart from those in your inner circle.

FOUR OF CUPS
Realm: The Sea

Emotional stability, self-soothing, caring for what truly matters, acceptance, emotional boundaries, prioritizing loved ones

In the past…
you poured your heart out, eager to experience love in all its forms. It was fun, but you soon found your own cup empty. So, you turned your love inward and a few special people followed, happy to reciprocate the gift of love they received from you.

At present…
your eyes lock with an axolotl floating contentedly in a delicate bubble. The soft pink glow pulsing around the bubble grows brighter, its light falling on your face. You are being allowed into the sanctuary of this gentle creature.

On the horizon…
a single beam of bright pink light shines up into the night sky, directing your eyes to stars and constellations you haven't noticed before. The source of the light is hidden but you know you must find it to find the focus of your heart.

From above…
warmth envelops you like a blanket and you relax into it, feeling safe and secure. As tension drains from your muscles, a clarity enters and you are filled with visions of exactly what feeds and what drains your heart.

Deep within…
your heart, an emotional reorganization is underway. You don't feel guilty when saying no to things you know aren't fulfilling to you. The relationships that matter most rise to the top and some others fall away effortlessly.

FOUR OF CUPS

FIVE OF CUPS

FIVE OF CUPS
Realm: The Sea

Emotional chaos, foreboding feelings, mood swings, release of emotional blockages, surprising reactions, uncomfortable vulnerability

In the past…
a wave of sadness and anger welled up in you without warning and without cause. You tried to push it down, but it was too powerful. Finally you found peace when you gave in and allowed the wave to sweep through you.

At present…
tree trunks crack as massive waves overwhelm their hold in the earth. Everything solid is swept away by the power of the water. Your emotions churn violently and threaten to break you apart. This storm came on suddenly and cannot be stopped.

On the horizon…
the placid sea swells under a darkening sky. The water in your body rises and falls, making you feel on edge and unsteady. You inhale the cool damp air, centering yourself in these moments of calm before the storm.

From above…
heavy rain falls suddenly from a clear blue sky. You try to take cover, but it is already too late, you are soaked through and knee deep in rising water. There is no time to understand, you can only allow the storm to pass through.

Deep within…
uncomfortable feelings pool in your stomach, then spill over to fill your entire body. These feelings are not in response to anything happening currently, they come from some time or lifetime before, finally demanding release here and now.

SIX OF CUPS
Realm: The Sea

Emotional maturity, acceptance, appreciation of all relationship lessons, development of healthy bonds, long-term friendships, overcoming emotional challenges

In the past…
you ran into an old friend walking through the park. As you sat together reminiscing and catching up on your lives, strangers smiled, recognizing the strength of your bond. You felt at peace knowing that keeping good friends means you are a good friend.

At present…
many years of photos of family and dear friends decorate your wall. You stop to look at them, revisiting the memories that made your relationships strong, and reflect with pride on the love and dedication that created your chosen family.

On the horizon…
friendly faces smile at you, floating on a calm sea. They are happy to see you, but in no hurry for you to reach them. They trust your kind heart and dependable nature and know you will make it in your own time.

From above…
a gentle rain breaks the heat of the day. You turn your face up to the sky and close your eyes to enjoy the feeling of the warm drops on your skin. Memories of gentle emotional cleansings surface in your happy heart.

Deep within…
there is a protective layer around your heart. This layer is not a defense created in response to emotional wounds, but rather a fortification built up over years of strong friendships and steady streams of love and commitment.

SIX OF CUPS

SEVEN OF CUPS

SEVEN OF CUPS
Realm: The Sea

Emotional breakthroughs, radical vulnerability, discovering true desires, expanding heart space, loving greatly, pushing through old barriers to giving and receiving love

In the past...
you were focused on what you thought you should want and so you couldn't feel what you actually desired in life until a kind friend acted as your mirror, reflecting back to you what you could not see on your own.

At present...
as you take in your reflection in a still pool, a glow forms around your heart. When you look down at your chest it isn't there. The glow is only for you to see reflected back to you, a message that your heart is bigger and brighter than you think.

On the horizon...
a new world is visible. It looks familiar, like you've seen it in a dream. There is a sadness for the time lost to not believing this world could be real, but it is overshadowed by the elation of knowing it exists.

From above...
cheers of greeting and celebration erupt. Revelers on a rooftop hold signs bearing your name and image and they excitedly urge you to join them. You had no idea you had such a positive effect on people, but it is undeniable, reflected here in their faces.

Deep within...
your heart a door is unlocked at last. Feelings flow freely through it and out into your body and mind. You are invigorated with new purpose and passion in life and love and begin to direct your energy accordingly.

EIGHT OF CUPS
Realm: The Sea

Matured emotional boundaries, understanding true nurturing, loving steadily, compassion, accepting one's own needs

In the past…
you exhausted yourself reading every book on relationships you could find, trying to follow all the rules and advice exactly. It didn't work until you added your own chapter, drawn from your own experience and tailored to your own needs.

At present…
penguins look on, unbothered, from an ice flow as a humpback whale breaches and sinks back into the Antarctic Ocean. The whale goes off in search of krill, the penguins continue their play, the serenity unbroken in this harsh and beautiful environment.

On the horizon…
the glacier comes into view. You pull your hat down and collar up against the biting cold wind, but you do not go inside. Here on the deck in the wind you can allow yourself to become enveloped in the expanse of white and blue and gray.

From above…
muffled sounds of a break on the surface barely make it to your ears. The whale's breach is dramatic from above, but here in the depths, the water remains still and constant, a steady zero degrees every day, reassuring and predictable.

Deep within…
you have grown to love yourself more than you ever thought possible. This love inspires you to set boundaries around which relationships and interactions you devote time and energy to and in what amounts.

EIGHT OF CUPS

NINE OF CUPS

NINE OF CUPS
Realm: The Sea

Expanding wisdom of the heart, emotional processing, growth and understanding, recognizing healthy relationships, developing coping and support skills

In the past…
a stranger's sigh stayed with you all day long, interrupting your thoughts as you tried in vain to figure out what feeling it conveyed. Was it sorrow? frustration? longing? Your obsession got you in touch with the wide diversity of emotions within yourself.

At present…
tears stream down your cheek carrying pain and confusion of the past out into open. A kind therapist facilitates deep insights and connections, giving you words to describe things you have never spoken of and can finally understand and release.

On the horizon…
the moon rises over the sea, shining its reflected light down onto a community of octopuses. As they interact with each other, their skin shifts in color and while you don't understand the exact meaning, the complexity of their expression impresses you.

From above…
tentacles reach down and pull you up from the sea floor and into the warm embrace of a giant octopus. You give a gentle pat to express your appreciation and your friend's skin flashes colors. Here in these tentacles, you always feel safe and loved.

Deep within…
disparate memories synthesize into precious insights into your emotional makeup. Understanding feelings from the past brings you peace in the present. You are ready to help others in their own personal discoveries and healing.

TEN OF CUPS
Realm: The Sea

Supportive community, freedom from shame, unconditional love, happiness, vicarious joy, security, family, open expression of emotion

In the past…
you often felt like an outsider in your community. Others seemed to gel effortlessly into groups while you looked on, confused, until someone sensed your need, took your hand and pulled you in. You were embraced and celebrated, forever changed.

At present…
holding hands, smiling up at the sun, you float in a circle of otters. Each of you has a different crystal resting on your heart, your unique contribution to the circle. You wiggle your toes and relax into this moment, cared for and carefree.

On the horizon…
cheering and laughter rise up among colorful streamers and fireworks. A grand celebration is underway and even from here its joyful energy is infectious. You make your way toward it, needing no invitation.

From above…
sunbeams filtered through the waves catch your eye and guide your attention up above your head where a school of rainbow fish is playing in the current, moving as one cohesive unit, beautifully connected in cheerful spirit.

Deep within…
you know that this is where you belong. You are accepted here for exactly who you are and where you are in your life. All fear of abandonment or rejection has melted away, leaving you free to accept and give love freely.

TEN OF CUPS

PAGE OF CUPS

PAGE OF CUPS
Realm: The Sea

Innocence, playfulness, vulnerability, renewal, emotional healing, a fresh start, forgiveness, purity of heart, joie de vivre

In the past...
your heart felt so battered and bruised that you closed off your emotions to protect yourself. A gentle being with an open heart came to your aid and helped to show you the strength and beauty in vulnerability, giving you a fresh start.

At present...
a school of small fish surrounds you as it passes, scales flashing in the light. It stops a few feet ahead and the small fish take the form of one big fish, gazing into a golden chalice, to discover the glory of love for the very first time.

On the horizon...
fish play with a golden chalice, batting it back and forth. As it moves through the water, the gold catches the light and reflects it in all directions like a slow-motion disco ball, adding to the lighthearted atmosphere and drawing other fish to the party.

From above...
shimmering fish dive down all around you like shooting stars. They circle your limbs and pull you into motion, making you dance like a marionette. You giggle, encouraging them, and your heart feels lighter than it has in ages.

Deep within...
your heart, a lifetime of sorrows is preparing to leave, taking all of their protective devices with them. They served you well, but now it's time to let them go. Your heart is healed and brave enough to come into the light again.

KNIGHT OF CUPS
Realm: The Sea

Passion, intensity, pride, loving freely, gallant expression of emotion, releasing shame, devotion to a cause, leading with the heart

In the past...
everything you loved, you loved passionately. You feared it was too much for others to handle, but your need to share your feelings was too intense to contain and you proudly stepped into the world with your heart on your sleeve.

At present...
a knight in jellyfish armor rides by on a seahorse, raising a chalice aloft to you in greeting. You see the knight greet everyone in this manner. In repetition, the gesture reads more as an announcement of an offering than a simple salutation.

On the horizon...
a figure comes into view, moving toward you, tentacles flowing wildly around it. You instinctively perk up and pay attention, waiting to receive whatever and whoever is coming your way, your heartbeat picking up speed in intense anticipation.

From above...
a golden cup floats down through the water and lands at your feet. You look up and your eyes meet the intense gaze of a knight who points at the cup and then at you and gives a little wink before riding away.

Deep within...
a passion for life and love bubbles in your heart and threatens to boil over. A strong sense of decorum keeps you from acting on your feelings but you're beginning to wonder whether following rules is worth stifling your emotional self.

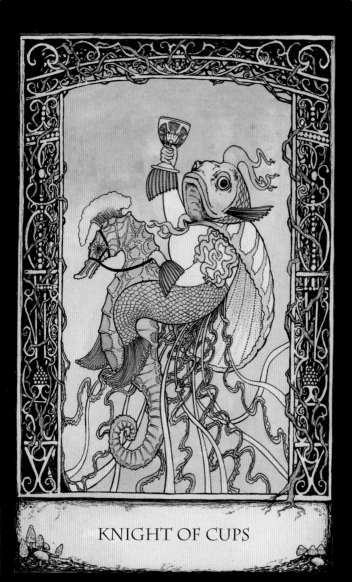

KNIGHT OF CUPS

QUEEN OF CUPS

QUEEN OF CUPS
Realm: The Sea

Compassion, emotional processing, cleansing old wounds, acceptance and release, surrender, separating the feeling from the memory

In the past...
waves of emotion rushed through you with such force you thought you might be ripped apart. The more you tried to stop them the more intense they got. You surrendered and immediately felt relief from the pain.

At present...
the Queen of the Sea is seated comfortably in a throne grown from the sea floor. The water is warm and calm, seaweed sways in a gentle current. The Queen offers a chalice to you, held at heart level and you humbly accept.

On the horizon...
great swells form as the tide rises. You can hear the rush of water and the power of it from miles away. Soon you will brave the depths, but for now, you sit and listen, acclimating to the rhythms of the sea.

From above...
you can see only a few feet beneath the surface of the lake. You reach your hand in to test the temperature and the water pulls you down into its dark depths. A crab scuttles out of the way as you gently land in this new world, ready to explore.

Deep within...
you feel yourself sinking down into your emotions. It is getting harder and harder to keep them contained. Down a hill, you see yourself reflected in a lake. You kick off your shoes, run down the dock, and jump in.

KING OF CUPS
Realm: The Sea

Understanding emotions, riding the waves, integrity, honesty, composure, seeing through overwhelming times to the relief ahead

In the past...
you found difficult conversations unbearable. Emotions overwhelmed you and clouded your thinking. Floating on a lake one summer day, you realized you could float on top of your feelings too, experiencing them without being consumed.

At present...
your heart is in your throat as you navigate through golden chalices laid out before the King of the Sea. When you arrive, your eyes lock and understanding passes between you, melting your anxiety and filling your heart with serenity.

On the horizon...
a bright blue light pulses in the center of a bubble floating on top of the water. The bubble rolls in the waves, but never floats up, it always maintains a connection with the water. The light dims and for a moment you think you see a figure in its glow.

From above...
water pressure compounds your turbulent emotions. A bubble descends from the surface to the sea floor and encapsulates you, then rises back up to the surface. You float there in the bubble, moving with the waves, calm and aware.

Deep within...
the connection between your head and your heart grows strong. Your emotional reactions are no longer confusing and you are able to strategize how to deal with similar situations in the future. You are learning to trust your heart again.

KING OF CUPS

ACE OF SWORDS

ACE OF SWORDS
Realm: The Sky

Divine truth, clarity, perfect communication, cutting through static, clearing distractions, conviction, sharp intellect, knowledge of purpose

In the past…
you felt as if you were perpetually surrounded by a thick fog, unable to understand the world around you. A sharp beam of light from the heavens cut through the fog and penetrated your mind, gifting you the ability to see with clarity.

At present…
birds chatter with excitement as they present a sword to you, descended from above. You accept, place your hand around the hilt, and inhale sharply, suddenly filled with a golden light beaming down into your body. The light of truth.

On the horizon…
an unearthly glow reaches up from behind the hilltops, lighting up the night sky. Puffs of gold dust grow thicker with each step you take, and you begin to recognize something deeply familiar in the light you can't quite yet place.

From above…
the sound of bells ringing pulls your attention upward, your ears and eyes open wide for the arrival of any information announced by the sound. A hawk catches your eye and a moment of understanding passes between you before it vanishes in the air.

Deep within…
an indistinct murmur grows in volume and insistence as you make your way up a steep hillside. At the top, you find a clearing and sit quietly, inviting the murmur to grow into a voice to share its wisdom with you.

TWO OF SWORDS
Realm: The Sky

A decision, an opening, new ways of thinking, the beginning of an intellectual pursuit, the evolution of language

In the past…
a withdrawal into your own mind gave you much-needed space to assess your options. With your eyes closed, wind rushing past your ears, a world within was revealed, containing all the answers you needed to make your choice.

At present…
two doors stand in a tree. You consider their color and shape and check for any sounds or smells coming from behind them. You can take your time, but you can only choose once, so you've got to gather as much information as possible.

On the horizon…
birds of all kinds flock together, forming a massive cloud of different colors and songs. The unusual nature of their meeting stops you in your tracks. Something is changing, new information is coming. A charge in the air stands your hair on end.

From above…
two voices call for your attention, but when you look up, there is no one to be seen, only empty windows in tall towers, their contrasting curtains billowing out in the wind like flags. Your mind quickly calculates which tower to investigate.

Deep within…
the experience and knowledge you've collected swirl together, forming new thoughts and opinions on your life. They create a shift in your consciousness, a need to make hard choices with this new information to open up your future.

TWO OF SWORDS

THREE OF SWORDS

THREE OF SWORDS
Realm: The Sky

Disagreement, conflicting opinions, unbalanced discussions, difficulty finding a clear right or wrong answer, the need to accept multiple viewpoints as valid

In the past…
a disagreement with friends threatened to tear your group apart. You tried to talk it out, but talking just made it worse. The only way to move forward was to stop talking at all. Silence and acceptance mended your bonds.

At present…
an argument erupts between an owl, an ostrich, and a swan. All argue their point passionately while never stopping to consider the very different perspectives of the others, formed by their lives in the sky, on land, and on water.

On the horizon…
dark clouds gather and animals scurry to take shelter. An eerie quiet fills the air. You study the sky, plotting a path that will keep you out of the worst of the storm while accepting a little discomfort is unavoidable.

From above…
a flash of lightning startles you into high alert. You look around to find potential sources of danger and instead see mostly places and people to shelter and protect you. Your guard comes down and you find yourself in easy conversation with new friends.

Deep within…
your memory, a pain you've tried to ignore is calling out to be heard. A channel of communication opens between your heart, your mind, and your past and a collaboration of understanding begins to unfold.

FOUR OF SWORDS
Realm: The Sky

New system of values, clarity of voice, stability in reasoning, intellectual conviction, bringing an avenue of inquiry to a satisfying conclusion

In the past...
late nights blended into early mornings over conversations about life, love, art, politics, and everything around and in between. These discussions helped you refine the solid convictions you hold now and established a framework for healthy debate.

At present...
a sense of peace settles in your mind and body as you inhale and exhale slowly, observing your breath. Your troubles seem small. The path to your goals is clear. Your priorities float effortlessly to the top of your consciousness.

On the horizon...
four apparitions appear, all versions of you. One of you is elegantly dressed for a formal affair, one carries supplies for an outing into the wilderness, one sits atop a pile of books, one wears pajamas, and only one of them can be your top priority.

From above...
a howling wind descends to clear the ground of debris, blowing the landscape clean and revealing the true nature of all you can see. You slowly turn to take in every view of the scene, surprised at how easy it is to see what is most important to you.

Deep within...
your understanding of the world has grown into a new alignment. Your values are clear and your conviction is strong. This is the foundation of your belief system, a ruler to measure and assess new information as it comes into your consciousness.

FOUR OF SWORDS

FIVE OF SWORDS

FIVE OF SWORDS
Realm: The Sky

Anxiety, confusion, stress, misunderstandings, not finding the right words, racing thoughts, crossed wires, isolation, the need to stop thinking

In the past...
strange mists clouded your vision, causing confusion and pain. They became thicker and thicker until you lost all sense of time and place. Deep inhales and purposeful exhales returned you to a place of calm, clear vision.

At present...
panic rises as your hands grasp for stability, catching nothing but the sting of debris as they pass through the sharp wind of the funnel cloud. A bird floats in the eye of the storm, calmly observing the chaos.

On the horizon...
the birds grow quiet and the air turns an eerie shade of green. Everything becomes still, even the ringing in your ears quiets down, as your whole body becomes an antenna, waiting to predict how the storm will affect you.

From above...
a chorus of whispering voices descends to invade your ears. Opinions, unwanted advice, judgments all swirl around you. You begin to hum a low constant tone that fills your body until it reaches all the way up to your head and quiets your mind.

Deep within...
messages from the past make their way through the labyrinth of your memory to bring their fears and insecurities to you in the present. They clutter your mind, blowing away reason and keeping you from seeing anything clearly.

SIX OF SWORDS
Realm: The Sky

Intellectual breakthroughs, problem solving, academic excellence, eloquence, recognition of accomplishment, accepting praise, speaking with grace

In the past…
an audience listened to you speak with rapt attention as you lectured passionately, offering your expert views and insights. Their minds opened, their thinking stretched, the power of your words changing them forever.

At present…
a broad smile stretches across your face as you think about all the late nights and long days, the supportive friends and generous teachers that got you here. Your name is called and you proudly step up to accept your diploma.

On the horizon…
a podium stands on an empty stage. People gather, chatting in groups before taking their seats. Someone tests the microphone, water is brought out and placed on the podium, programs are handed out. Everything is set for you to share your knowledge.

From above…
garlands of flowers float softly down, coloring and scenting the air. You catch one around your neck like it's a carnival game and wear it the rest of the day as a symbol of your pride in your accomplishments.

Deep within…
your voice waits patiently to be honored for the wisdom it carries. Years of lessons synthesized into theories and intellectual hypotheses are stored, invaluable contributions to public discourse, all hard-won accomplishments.

SIX OF SWORDS

SEVEN OF SWORDS

SEVEN OF SWORDS
Realm: The Sky

Mental breakthroughs, unexpected advances in communication, finding the missing piece to a puzzle, rising to the occasion, speaking in prose

In the past…
your shoulder trembled as you drew back the bow, your muscles having limited memory and experience. You released the arrow and held your breath as it raced to land in the tiny bullseye in the distance.

At present…
flying above the treetops, you take in the vast scale and beauty of the landscape. An opening in the clouds sends sunlight streaming through, lighting up the entrance to another level of splendor above the clouds.

On the horizon…
the tops of carnival tents are just visible, the sounds of the arcade echoing in the valley. The bells and shouts bring up memories of frustration and ignite a competitive streak within you. You are determined to prove your skill.

From above…
crackling sounds like branches breaking startle you. You duck for cover and look up to see no trees or branches falling, but the sky itself breaking open to give you access to new heights and dimensions of understanding.

Deep within…
aspirations you've held secretly for years are stirring, flexing against their containers, threatening to break free. You start to say them out loud, gaining support from friends and making a pact with yourself to plot your path to success.

EIGHT OF SWORDS
Realm: The Sky

Formalized communication, established paradigms, long-term correspondence, friendly rapport, comfortable patterns of thinking, a steady tone of voice

In the past...
you reached out to a friend you hadn't spoken to in a while, nervously anticipating a change in the relationship. Instead, your effort was appreciated and you found your bond to be even stronger with the passing of time.

At present...
an arctic tern makes its journey down the length of the globe, the longest migratory path of any species on earth. For the tern, this is not an heroic undertaking, it is simply how life is lived, a logical path taken for simple necessity.

On the horizon...
the summer sun dips down in the arctic sky, the start of a brilliant sunset that will last for weeks before the sun finally disappears beneath the horizon for the winter. You settle in to gaze at the colors and take out a notebook and pen.

From above...
the shrill calls of a colony of terns snaps you to attention. You watch them depart to the next stop on their journey. As they grow distant, you see your future in the clouds, a vision of your life stretching into the distance.

Deep within...
the armature of your belief system holds up your convictions and guides your moral compass. This internal support allows you to have more respect and understanding for others whose views differ from your own and makes difficult conversations a bit easier.

EIGHT OF SWORDS

NINE OF SWORDS

NINE OF SWORDS
Realm: The Sky

Advanced understanding, knowing what you don't know, true acceptance of the reality of others, evolution of thought, intellectual wisdom, integration of knowledge

In the past…
you were widely regarded as an expert in your field, respected and admired for your intellectual accomplishments. Still, you pushed further, knowing that there is always more to discover beyond the limits of present understanding.

At present…
you sit in the central hall of a massive library. Your gaze travels from your stack of books, up the shelves to the stained glass windows and you marvel at all the knowledge you have acquired and all you will never know.

On the horizon…
a massive stone building rises into the sky. Flocks of birds circle the spire in celebration of the divine nature of this temple of knowledge. Through the windows, you can just make out shelves of books extending all the way to the ceiling.

From above…
a rush of wind rustles the pages of your book, causing you to lose your page. When you lift your hand your eyes are drawn to a single word. It reverberates in your mind and you set down your book to consider all that it means.

Deep within…
air fills your lungs, sending a feeling of expansion up your throat and into your mind. You smile, excited to follow your curiosity to fill this space with new knowledge and experiences and to see how your wisdom will grow and change.

TEN OF SWORDS
Realm: The Sky

Completion, drawing conclusions, having considered all options, the logical end of conversation, assurance that nothing has been left unsaid

In the past...
you had a problem. After many hours of thorough thought and research, you found the best solution. But then you second-guessed yourself, searching for more answers, until you finally returned to your original solution, vowing to trust yourself in the future.

At present...
a skein of geese fly overhead in formation, taking turns at the lead to make wind resistance easier for the rest of the group. It's a simple solution, one that works well for everyone. You look back to your assembled group and move to close the debate.

On the horizon...
sunlight is beginning to glow, coloring the clouds bright orange, invigorating and warm. This dawn promises the closure of dusk at the end of the day. You look forward to it, taking comfort in the certainty of the cycle.

From above...
wind whistles through the treetops in a natural orchestral performance. The sound swells and retreats, grows faster and slower, always moving, always changing, and yet always remaining a perfectly steady presence to quiet your mind.

Deep within...
a stillness anchors you in your body and empties your mind. You have done all of the thinking and all of the talking you can do. Now it is time to simply be, accepting the truth and looking forward to the next chapter.

TEN OF SWORDS

PAGE OF SWORDS

PAGE OF SWORDS
Realm: The Sky

Unfiltered truth, honesty, curiosity, playing with meaning, updating old language, accurate observations, unconventional ideas

In the past…
you looked in the mirror and saw someone else's face. The face of a person who did their best, who met challenges with grace and spoke with gentle honesty. All your self-critical language evaporated, replaced by a new language of appreciation.

At present…
a flock of little birds surrounds you in song. They move as one, dancing in the sunlight, and arrange themselves into one large bird. It picks a sword up from the ground, a flood of recognition and revelation flashes across its eyes.

On the horizon…
birds gather in such great numbers, they block out the sun, creating an avian solar eclipse. You sit in the dim light and clear your mind, grateful for the reset, ready to form a new, kinder vocabulary.

From above…
the beating of wings creates a wind that blows through your mind, clearing out all the ways you speak to yourself that keep you small and afraid. You are lighter, so light you float up to fly with the birds.

Deep within…
a vibration like the fluttering of tiny wings grows in your mind, shaking loose old outdated ways of thinking and sweeping them away. Your body feels more solid, your vision true and clear, free of the veils of assumption.

KNIGHT OF SWORDS
Realm: The Sky

Speaking passionately, advocacy, direct communication, potential for harsh words, conviction, quick reactions, rapid processing of information

In the past…
you kept your opinions quiet to avoid upsetting anyone. It left your throat and stomach burning. A bluejay darted down at you, defending its territory. Inspired by the fearlessness of this small bird, you vowed to speak your mind.

At present…
a bluejay expertly commands a much larger bird while holding a sword aloft as if flying into battle, though there is no enemy in sight. The intensity of the jay, prepared to fight at a moment's notice, is thrilling and a little frightening.

On the horizon…
a hawk carrying a flaming stick in its beak, draws patterns and symbols in the sky in smoke. You stand in rapt attention, trying to translate the writing, but it blows away too quickly. Irritated, you will the hawk to repeat the message.

From above…
a wind blows so swiftly that you have to bend and extend your arms to keep from falling over. Debris pelts your face. You close your eyes and mouth tight until your frustration boils over and you open your mouth to scream.

Deep within…
your brain, your synapses are firing at lightning speed, formulating and refining your ideas about the world and your place within it. Internal debates happen instantaneously, conclusions arrive effortlessly, demanding to be spoken out loud.

KNIGHT OF SWORDS

QUEEN OF SWORDS

QUEEN OF SWORDS
Realm: The Sky

Words of affirmation, speaking from the heart, the language of love, openness, a rosy outlook, smoothing things over, finding common ground

In the past…
you spoke with a studied pragmatism, careful not to let your feelings color your thoughts and opinions, thinking this would make you less of an intellectual. Your heart rebelled and demanded you speak her language, breaking you free.

At present…
you stand before the Queen of the Air, a glorious bird decked out in feathered finery. You lock eyes and your nervousness floats away. The queen holds a sword out to you at heart level. You touch it and your mind fills with love.

On the horizon…
sailboats dot the coastline with color, bobbing cheerfully in the waves. They look like a group of good friends engaged in conversation, everyone included and heard. You link arms with your friends and pull them close.

From above…
the humid air seems to press down on you. You move slowly to a hammock tied between two trees and gratefully settle in, swinging yourself to create a slight breeze, with nothing to do but listen to your heart.

Deep within…
your heart, a voice calls out to you. It is so quiet you have to be perfectly still to hear it, turning all of your attention inward. This is what the voice has been waiting for, these moments alone, just you and your heart.

KING OF SWORDS
Realm: The Sky

Intellect, strategy, rationality, structured thinking, logic, presenting a sound argument, clarity of mind and voice, refinement, analysis

In the past…
you closely studied the theories of others, but had trouble forming your own point of view. You were too close. You needed distance to see how the intersections of all these trains of thought fit together, where they clashed, and what you found in the pattern.

At present…
your clothes flap lightly in the wind as the King of Air assesses your character, sword aloft, an antenna to gather divine communications. The sword descends, the King touches its tip to the top of your head. You are anointed.

On the horizon…
kites glide gracefully through the sky, brought to life by a perfect breeze on a clear day. You trace the random paths they take with your eyes, retaining the patterns and shapes, and make a game of creating a language from them.

From above…
a funnel cloud drops down and grabs you, pulling you up into the air. You find you can float safely in the sky and you relax, taking in the vast landscape above and below the clouds, understanding both are your home.

Deep within…
your mind's eye, guided by your breath, you reach a state of peace. In this meditative state, you keep just one question in your consciousness. When you open your eyes, the answer arrives, as if switched on like a lightbulb.

KING OF SWORDS

ACE OF COINS

ACE OF COINS
Realm: The Forest and Mountains

Divine material, planting a golden seed, unlimited potential for building, alignment of mundane and divine goals, merging of the physical and spiritual selves

In the past…
you needed to have a full plan in place before you started to build anything, filling notebooks with fragments of ideas that never took form. A little golden seed fell into your lap. You planted it and watched as it grew, needing no one to tell it what to be.

At present…
beetles work diligently to unearth a golden coin. It gleams in the sunlight, blinding you momentarily, and your mind becomes a blank slate. The beetles finish their work and you pick up the coin, ready to build your empire from the ground up.

On the horizon…
the ground emits a golden glow bright enough to be seen in the afternoon sun. A steady parade of insects travels toward it, as if making a pilgrimage en masse. You stand up straighter, your body an extension of this holy ground.

From above…
bright golden light shines down on you, making your body appear shimmery and incandescent. You examine your arms and the backs of your hands, amazed that you live in this physical form, then turn your hands over to find a small coin resting in your palm.

Deep within…
your body, a sense of solidity anchors you to the Earth, allowing you to reach further out into the universe without fear. You hold the power to build anything you need in this life and the wisdom to know what to build and where to begin.

TWO OF COINS
Realm: The Forest and Mountains

New growth, emergence of form, seeing the potential in a project, fostering organic development, allowing room for change, taking first steps

In the past…
a sense of urgency permeated your life. Anything you began to build could be easily discarded if you didn't see immediate results. Once you developed patience and stopped pushing so hard, things began to build much more quickly and easily.

At present…
you look on as a massive bear waters a tiny sprout, shielding it with its body and being careful to pour the water slowly from the watering can so as to not overwhelm the young plant, fiercely protecting and nurturing in equal measure.

On the horizon…
a light rain falls on a freshly tilled field. You inhale the smell of the soil and feel a rush through your body as endless possibilities of what could grow there race through your mind, then reach into your pocket and find a handful of seeds.

From above…
seed pods float gently to the ground. When they land, they sprout instantly into tiny shoots that quickly cover the ground all around you and open into a wide variety of plants. You contentedly wait to see what they will become.

Deep within…
a sense of what is taking shape develops as you work clay in your hands. You quiet your mind, trusting your fingers to find the form this piece of clay needs to become at this time and place under your care.

TWO OF COINS

THREE OF COINS

THREE OF COINS
Realm: The Forest and Mountains

Collaboration, recognizing your strengths and weaknesses, conflict resolution, large-scale building, diverse talents and skills, multiple expert opinions

In the past…
you were hard at work on a project, head down, frustrated, needing another skilled hand, but afraid to be a bother. A gentle tap on your shoulder and a cheerful request for your help was not a bother at all, but an honor, one you soon reciprocated.

At present…
three raccoons in a cloak sneak into an orchard. The bottom raccoon carries the weight of the group and walks, the middle one holds the balance and the basket, and the top reaches up to pluck the best fruit from the tree. A perfect team.

On the horizon…
a monument is being built. Mules pull carts of materials, laborers sort and distribute the materials, builders secure them in place, and architects and designers oversee the construction. It is an impressive and efficient ecosystem.

From above…
an apple falls on your head. You look up to see three raccoons in a cape staring at you, frozen. You smile and they relax and go back to stealing apples. The ripest fruit is just out of their reach and you stand and reach up to help.

Deep within…
an understanding and acceptance of your strengths and capabilities is growing and clarifying. You do not need to do everything or be good at everything. What you have to offer is valuable and impressive right here and now.

FOUR OF COINS
Realm: The Forest and Mountains

Material stability, having basic needs met, establishing healthy routines, finding what brings you security, cutting out excess

In the past…
you kept yourself afloat juggling odd jobs and irregular hours. It was exhausting, so you developed wellness routines that fit into your life to keep yourself grounded. These rituals were the first step in putting down roots of stability.

At present…
a squirrel chatters happily outside the door of a simple little house high in a tree. The house is perfect for the squirrel and you are reminded that there is no universal standard for wealth or happiness. We all make our own.

On the horizon…
boulders dot the base of a mountain range. At first you think they fell into place naturally, but as night falls lights begin to shine from spaces between them and you see they are houses made from the materials closest at hand.

From above…
a rustling in the leaves of a tall oak draws your attention to a flurry of activity in the treetops. A squirrel has abandoned its nest and is gathering sticks and breaking them down to build a sturdy house.

Deep within…
energetic roots connect your body to the depths of the Earth. You close your eyes and feel these roots draw up all of the energy you need while sending any excess back down to be transmuted and recycled.

FOUR OF COINS

FIVE OF COINS

FIVE OF COINS
Realm: The Forest and Mountains

Scarcity mentality, disruption of supplies, a need to reallocate resources, destabilization, conservation, doing more with less, fixation on absence, fear of lack

In the past...
you counted every penny, made do with the absolute least and squirreled everything else away, constantly stressed about the future. Your savings grew, but your happiness did not. Life passed you by until you learned to trust yourself with money.

At present...
you reach into your pockets and find nothing but sand. As it runs through your fingers, your head falls, heavy with disappointment. A deafening rumble cuts through you as a rock face collapses in a landslide flowing in your direction.

On the horizon...
a bluff reaches so high that wispy clouds float past its edge and mature trees at its base look like saplings. A rock falls down the cliffside, then another and another. You sense the whole thing is about to crash down on the forest below.

From above...
wind in the tree branches sounds like hungry ghosts howling in the night. You lower your head and try to ignore it, focusing on the ground. An apple tree laden with perfectly ripe fruit stands near, waiting for you to lift your gaze.

Deep within...
a hollow rumbling echoes through your body making you aware of everything you do not contain. The rumbling is so loud it is hard to focus on anything else. You cannot even recognize your own keen inner hearing for the gift it is.

SIX OF COINS
Realm: The Forest and Mountains

Clear accomplishments, seeing results, material gains, triumph over physical obstacles, feats of strength, building for the future on the foundation of the past

In the past…
though you could barely walk a mile without becoming exhausted, you decided to climb a mountain. You conditioned your mind and body, pushing a little further every day. The view from the top of the mountain was the most beautiful thing you'd ever seen.

At present…
as you gaze out over a mountain range, you pause to look back over how far you've come. Seeing the trail wind back down the mountain and through the clouds, your chest swells with pride in all the work and training it took to get you here.

On the horizon…
you can see the trailhead marker at the base of a mountain. The sky is clear and a slight breeze cools your skin. You check your supplies one last time and take a few moments to steady your nerves before setting out.

From above…
the sun shines on your face and the ground supports you while you lie in a field of wildflowers. You close your eyes and feel the blood pumping through your heart, the power of your body and its connection with the Earth.

Deep within…
the cells of your body, the memories of your accomplishments live. They are not isolated occurrences of the past, but rather integral parts of your being and identity. You feel these living memories lift you up as you navigate the world and its challenges.

SIX OF COINS

SEVEN OF COINS

SEVEN OF COINS
Realm: The Forest and Mountains

Physical transformation, breakthroughs in health, a new era of building, transformation of material world, recognition of heightened skills, development made apparent

In the past...
you grew increasingly frustrated with yourself. Materials felt awkward in your hands, the learning curve seemed impossibly steep. You had to walk away. When you returned to your project, you were amazed to find your hands suddenly had the dexterity of an expert.

At present...
autumn leaves crunch beneath your feet as you make your way toward a large circle made of sticks. A fox sits smiling at the entrance and beyond you can see the forest in spring, an accelerated development of natural processes.

On the horizon...
a gust of wind scatters dry leaves as the light grows dim. You take a deep breath, preparing yourself for the coming winter. A spot of bright green catches your eye, the door to spring already opening and your muscles relax.

From above...
brown leaves fall from trees glowing orange, yellow, and red. As they dance in the air on their way to the ground, you marvel at how many colors they display in their short lives, so much physical transformation in so little time.

Deep within...
your body, even while you sleep, an endless orchestration of change takes place. Cells multiply, your blood responds to conditions in the body, oxygen is extracted from air leaving carbon dioxide to be exhaled. All with no conscious effort from you.

EIGHT OF COINS
Realm: The Forest and Mountains

Established wealth, a stable and supportive home, steady work, a well-functioning system, operational procedures, safety rules and regulations, natural processes, slow and steady wins the race

In the past…
you changed your methods often, searching for a better, faster way to get things done. It ended up costing you more time and effort than you saved, so you chose one modality and stuck to it, letting it develop naturally over time.

At present…
giant sequoias tower over you, blocking out the sun with their massive forms. These trees are thousands of years old. They have weathered and witnessed millennia of change, as they lived and grew in their own steady manner.

On the horizon…
an ancient forest dominates the landscape. You see a deer standing near one of the trunks and are shocked to realize how massive the trees are. A deep respect for the wisdom of the forest settles in your body.

From above…
tiny shafts of light make their way through the dense canopy of the forest, illuminating the soft, thick bark of the sequoias. You look up to the treetops, cool and safe in the shelter they provide here on the ground.

Deep within…
your bones lives the memory of all the generations who came before you. The lessons of thousands of grandparents, their strengths and weaknesses and adaptations, are an integral part of how you experience the world and how you move through it.

EIGHT OF COINS

NINE OF COINS

NINE OF COINS
Realm: The Forest and Mountains

Higher education, experiential learning, building understanding, walking in the shoes of others, pushing beyond personal limits, collective evolution of skills

In the past...
you were hesitant to venture outside the known limits of your skill set. The thought of failure was terrifying. But the boredom of repetition finally overtook that fear and you ventured out of your comfort zone to try new things and embrace your mistakes.

At present...
a colony of termites has abandoned their usual mound construction to build a scale replica of the Roman aqueducts, an impressively ambitious undertaking to expand the growth potential of their colony. They push forward, brick by brick, without hesitation.

On the horizon...
a flurry of activity animates the landscape as animals gather building materials, racing the setting sun. They take turns examining and then demonstrating how each of the materials can be used to make a shelter that meets the needs of all.

From above...
woodchips fall from high in a tree where a woodpecker is hard at work. You take a few steps back and shield your eyes from the sun. A portrait of yourself made of hundreds of little holes is taking shape. The woodpecker puffs up its chest with pride.

Deep within...
the Earth, the ground rumbles, opening up a crack in the surface. You look over the edge of the crack and find a chest full of books and tools, a treasure of new skills to learn and practice.

TEN OF COINS
Realm: The Forest and Mountains

Abundant community, sharing resources, celebration of friendship, healthy society, diversity of strengths, pitching in, opening doors

In the past…
you lingered on the edges, never feeling like you fit in. Loneliness pushed you to overcome your fear of rejection. When you did, you found you had a comfortable and appreciated role to play in the happiness of the group.

At present…
all of the animals of the forest feast together at a grand banquet. The table is covered with more than enough foods to please the diversity of tastes. Throughout the party, animals continue to arrive carrying their own contributions.

On the horizon…
banners and streamers fill the sky above a dancing crowd. Music is punctuated by the pop of champagne corks followed by cheers and smoke rises from a large grill. You cannot help but smile. The pure joy is infectious.

From above…
on the hillside, sounds of jubilation roll down into your ears. Singing, laughter, and the clinking of glasses draw you in and pull you toward the celebration. You stop to gather a bouquet of flowers on the way, not wanting to arrive empty handed.

Deep within…
you know your needs will always be provided for because you provide for others. You do this not out of obligation, but because it truly brings you joy to see your whole community thriving, lifting each other as you rise together.

TEN OF COINS

PAGE OF COINS

PAGE OF COINS
Realm: The Forest and Mountains

Back to basics, new ways of building, a fresh foundation, getting grounded in the body, connection with the natural world, throwing out old blueprints

In the past…
you obsessively poured over decades of plans and research to determine why nothing you built stayed standing. A spider worked diligently on an intricate web, so delicate, yet holding together in a stiff breeze. You set down your plans to watch and learn.

At present…
ants stream in from all around, carrying bits of material to build one giant ant. The giant ant holds a large golden coin, regarding it with curiosity. The small ants arrange themselves to strengthen the giant ant, deftly responding to changing physical needs.

On the horizon…
a variety of building materials are arranged in neat piles. Groups and individuals come and go, taking what they need. You try to guess what they are building based on their choices, your own ideas growing and expanding with each guess.

From above…
dust floats down to settle on your arms and face. Its weight feels comforting as it accumulates, like it's holding you in your body and holding your body to the ground. You stay still until it covers you completely, then burst out, reborn.

Deep within…
the solid core of your being breaks into little pieces, arranging and rearranging themselves to be anything and everything while remaining completely you. This infinite adaptability awakens your curiosity and helps you see the endless possibilities you hold.

KNIGHT OF COINS
Realm: The Forest and Mountains

Giving form to passion, Earth magick, a need to bring something tangible into the world, practical creativity, launching a project or business

In the past…
you tried hard to do what you thought you should, following rules and advice that worked for others. Nothing really came of it. You wished you could make a good life for yourself and in that moment you saw your own definition of good, your true desire.

At present…
walking in a tunnel, you are stopped by a smartly dressed shrew riding an armadillo. The shrew says you can pass if you answer one question: If you could create any physical thing in the world, alone, what would it be?

On the horizon…
the entrance to a cave looms, guarded by a squadron of rodents dressed for battle. The guards are docile until provoked, fiercely protective of their home. You admire their fervor, your hand instinctively reaching into your pocket to grip a powerful stone you carry from your homeland.

From above…
the thunderous sound of giant footsteps fills a cavern, rattling everything inside. Bats depart their roosts and a few stalactites detach and fall to the floor. Young shrews pick them up and use them as makeshift swords to practice their fencing.

Deep within…
your body, a molten core churns. It centers your gravity and heats you from within. You put your hand on your abdomen to feel its glow and are filled with inspiration to build the life you desire from the ground up.

KNIGHT OF COINS

QUEEN OF COINS

QUEEN OF COINS
Realm: The Forest and Mountains

Nurturing growth, development of assets, making a house a home, meaningful gifts, offering support, love made manifest, cultivating a solid foundation

In the past...
you rationed out your love, afraid it might run out. It was lonely and unfulfilling. Little by little you opened your heart, allowing yourself to love your body, your home, your work. Your love only increased as you poured it out, creating a thriving, joyful life.

At present...
nestled in a throne of crystals, feet in a bed of feathers, the Queen of Earth gazes kindly upon you over her golden coin. You bow respectfully and feel the coin touch your head. When you look up, everything sparkles with new radiance.

On the horizon...
a mob of meerkats stands upright, eyeing you suspiciously. You sit to make yourself smaller. Two of the mob stay standing as lookouts while the others go about their hunting. You bow slightly to show your admiration and deference to their territorial claim.

From above...
rain falls down on the bare earth, creating a field of mud. You happily sink further and further into the mud, thinking of yourself as a seed being planted and nurtured into growing into your most abundant form.

Deep within...
the ground beneath your feet, your heart beats with the heart of the Earth. You work together, in collaboration, to create a sustainable world that supports the needs of all. One day and one brick at a time.

KING OF COINS
Realm: The Forest and Mountains

Strategic use of resources, recognizing value, cultivating talent, planning for the future, consideration of ecosystems, seeing the big picture

In the past…
the stone you wanted to use to build your cottage became unavailable. You were devastated, but begrudgingly tried using different materials. They worked even better, expanding your creative vision and the quality of your work.

At present…
the King of Earth regards you coolly, nose twitching, regal coat rooted in a great pile of golden coins. Everything in the royal burrow is as beautiful as it is essential, every stone and root a vital contribution to the whole of the environment.

On the horizon…
the morning mist lifts, giving you a full view of the valley below. Smoke rises from chimneys of cottages, cattle graze in the pastures, birds stir in the trees. Your mind is completely calm and clear, the future wide open.

From above…
a great canopy is unfurled as trumpets announce the arrival of a dignitary. Sun shining through the fabric casts a golden glow on the crowded, joyful street below. Everyone and everything appears well cared for in this idyllic community.

Deep within…
the worries and doubts that have plagued you for years have vanished. When you imagine your future, you see endless possibilities where you once saw hazardous obstacles. You are confident you have what you need to build your ideal life.

KING OF COINS

ACE OF WANDS

ACE OF WANDS
Realm: The Desert and Volcanoes

Divine creation, action, intuition, willpower, manifestation, magickal abilities, spiritual purification of the will, the innate power to conjure one's own life

In the past...

you seemed to stumble into situations you feared or dreaded. You thought you were cursed, but really anything you focused on came to you. Once you fixed your attention on what you wanted to attract instead of what you feared, you embraced your immense power.

At present...

dragons revel at the mouth of a volcano as lava bursts forth and flows in a river of fire. A wand is born, a singular magickal wand created just for you, fitted to your hand and imbued with powers only you can wield.

On the horizon...

fire erupts from a volcano, sending streams of lava down onto the land below. The sky turns bright orange and you feel a pulse of energy run through your body as a magnetic force pulls you toward the action.

From above...

drops of lava fall in a circle around you that sets the ground aflame. You back away, startled, until you realize the circle of fire is a protective wall enclosing a space for your indoctrination into the sacred magick of Fire.

Deep within...

your soul, an unseen force keeps you aware of the limitless possibilities of your life in this world. If you can imagine it, you can conjure it, through a combination of your own power and the support of the divine universe.

TWO OF WANDS
Realm: The Desert and Volcanoes

Opening up of options, a change in direction, choosing a path, listening to your intuition, letting a process evolve, merging of creative powers

In the past…
you sat at a crossroads, waiting for someone to come along and tell you where the roads led and which way to take. You sat for hours, but no one came. When it started getting dark, you stood and simply walked down the path you were facing.

At present…
you stand at the center of a fork in the road, studying your map. This intersection is not notated. You fold the map and put it away. Seeing no reason to avoid either direction, you follow your first step down an uncharted path.

On the horizon…
massive boulders pile up before high red cliffs. You cannot see around them or travel through them. Up ahead, the path divides and you'll have to choose to go around the left or right, not knowing where either way leads.

From above…
the beating of leathery wings lights up your excitement. A dragon is near. You scan the sky, but see nothing. The sound repeats, seemingly from two different directions. With no time to think, you run toward one to try to catch a glimpse of the beast.

Deep within…
you feel a pull. It is not yet clear what you are being pulled toward or away from, but you know an opportunity for change is coming soon. You consider your priorities now, knowing when decision time comes, you will need to trust your instinct.

TWO OF WANDS

THREE OF WANDS

THREE OF WANDS
Realm: The Desert and Volcanoes

Creative collectives, the need to make a new path, venturing into new territory, collaboration with the elements and the universe

In the past...
you worked in your studio day and night, perfecting your technique. Your craftsmanship was beyond compare, but your pieces lacked feeling. You called on some artist friends for input and their contributions transformed your work and your process.

At present...
a fennec fox climbs out of the den it has shared for so long and scouts for a place to refresh. It begins to dig, using all the knowledge and experience gained from life in previous dens to create a masterpiece of comfort and functionality.

On the horizon...
columns of flame shoot up from the ground for a few seconds randomly and without warning, making the terrain ahead dangerous to cross. There is no sure safe path. You will have to trust your timing and your route and make a run for it.

From above...
a rush of wind and crack of lightning foretell the coming rain. You plant your feet firmly on the ground and open yourself to the powers of Air, Fire, Water, and Earth to gather your magick in preparation for casting your spell.

Deep within...
you can feel that an alchemical process is taking place inside you, bringing together your experiences, your willpower, your desires, and your connection to the natural and spiritual worlds to conjure your personal form of magick.

FOUR OF WANDS
Realm: The Desert and Volcanoes

Creative agility, finding comfort in change, adaptability, going with the flow, mastering the basics, applying consistent abilities to evolving situations

In the past...
in times of uncertainty, you moved slowly, taking one careful, shaky step after another. You believed this kept you safer, even as it prolonged your precarious position. In desperation, you ran ahead, your balance and footing strengthened by your movement.

At present...
you make your way across a lava field, jumping carefully from rock to rock. If you are too careful, you start to lose your balance. You've got to be quick to be sure on your feet, trusting your intuition on which rock to jump to next.

On the horizon...
a boiling river stands between you and your destination. You take in the scene, noting the rocks that dot the surface and how the river flows around some and over others. You shift your weight back and forth to prepare for your crossing.

From above...
flashing lights disorient you. You stumble and bend your knees to catch yourself from falling. Loud music plays and as you tune into it, moving your body to the beat, you become solid and balanced with the constant motion of your dancing.

Deep within...
you have always craved change. Your restlessness moves you across countries and inspires you to try everything that you can at least once. You are not running from anything. This is where you are most comfortable, where you feel most yourself.

FOUR OF WANDS

FIVE OF WANDS

FIVE OF WANDS
Realm: The Desert and Volcanoes

False starts, mixed messages, unintended and unforeseen consequences, lack of motivation, creative blocks, inability to act, lack of trust in oneself

In the past…
in the middle of a big project on a tight deadline, a creative rut hit you. You tried taking a walk, listening to music, pushing yourself harder. Nothing worked to reignite your spark. You ceded control to the universe and set down your work until it returned.

At present…
a fire tears through the wilderness, leaving a trail of destruction. Inhabitants rush to safety and comfort one another, unable to stop it, not knowing when it will end, relying only on radical acceptance and a deep appreciation for what is left standing.

On the horizon…
large clouds of black smoke fill the sky. The air around you has an eerie orange glow and a sour smell. You cover your face with a scarf and squint your eyes, looking for the safest place to wait out the fire.

From above…
ash falls like snow from the sky, blocking the sun and covering everything in a layer of gray. Your stomach drops and your shoulders curl in as your body anticipates the unseen danger burning nearby and seeks its own protection.

Deep within…
the voice that usually guides you is silent. There is no inner knowing, no instinct for direction, no urge for creative expression. Even physical movement seems impaired as your actions don't have the results you've come to expect.

SIX OF WANDS
Realm: The Desert and Volcanoes

Creative triumph, successful solutions, winning a race, honing your instincts, realizing your magick has been working all along

In the past…
an idea for a creation possessed you. You did not have the expertise or the materials to pull it off, but you willed them to come to you and practiced your art every day until you were prepared to bring your dream to life.

At present…
you put the final touches on your masterpiece, taking your time and enjoying this last stage of the process. When you began, your work was unrefined and it fills you with satisfaction to see how far your skills have come.

On the horizon…
a wide open field calls to you. As you walk toward it, you encounter trinkets from your past, emblems of plans gone right and successful manifestations. You stop to remember each one, gathering confidence to embark on your biggest project yet.

From above…
voices cheering bring a smile to your face and warmth to your heart. You look up to find where they are and who they are cheering for and see many previous versions of yourself, all rooting for you and proud of all you've done.

Deep within…
confidence in your powers grows with each successful spell. Magick courses through your veins, your positivity and belief are infectious. Like-minded people, working to make the world a better place for all, are drawn into your orbit.

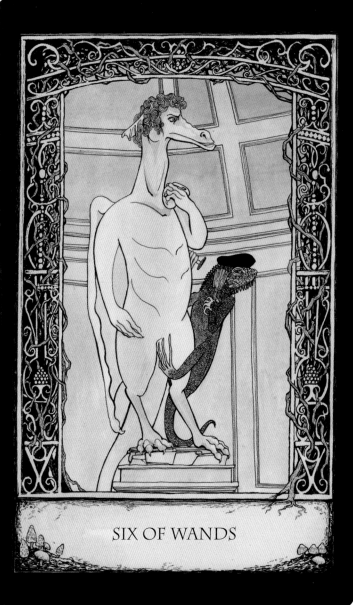

SIX OF WANDS

SEVEN OF WANDS

SEVEN OF WANDS
Realm: The Desert and Volcanoes

Magickal breakthroughs, finding a shortcut, creating a portal, channeled creations, pushing past known limits, breaking records

In the past…
you accepted your reality as constant and singular. Closing your eyes to imagine what could have been, you felt yourself floating and looked down to see your old world far beneath you, the portal to a new one opening above.

At present…
alone in the desert, exhausted and parched, you are thrilled when a camel approaches, thinking it will carry you to safety. Instead, it conjures a circle of flame and jumps through into a lush oasis. You follow, directing your will into your hands to conjure your own portal.

On the horizon…
green light flashes in the clouds beyond the hills. It is unlike any color you've ever seen in nature. The clouds move toward you, but when they pass the hills the flash disappears. You strain your eyes to look for a way through to this other world.

From above…
blinding light fills the sky and you squeeze your eyes shut to protect them. When the light dims enough for you to open your eyes again, you are in a different plane, a blank slate. A wand appears in your hand and you begin to create your world.

Deep within…
you can tell you are different than you were yesterday. Doubt is removed, your power unimpeded. There is a buzzing throughout your being that makes you feel capable and ready, excited to meet any challenges that come your way.

EIGHT OF WANDS
Realm: The Desert and Volcanoes

Virtuosic artistic skills, rehearsed performance, established creative practice, maximum productivity without burnout, running a marathon

In the past…
you experimented with many mediums and styles of art to find how to best express yourself, but became frustrated by your skill level not matching your vision. Once you found a form that really clicked, mastery developed steadily with regular practice.

At present…
a band of musicians come together to play in the desert. Their joy is as intoxicating as their music and their clear affection for one another. The music plays continuously, transitioning seamlessly from song to song as only great performers can do.

On the horizon…
lights shine from the windows of tall buildings and modest cafes, illuminating the bustling city life. You can see bright murals on the walls and hear conversation, music, traffic, cheering, all coming together in a thriving creative culture.

From above…
a cacophony of sound fills your ears as a brass band tunes up to play on a balcony high above the sidewalk. The musicians launch into an improvised number, catching the attention of passersby who stop to dance in the street.

Deep within…
your passion to create is unwavering. You don't feel like yourself unless you express yourself in art every day. A small drawing, a song, one page in a book you are writing, it doesn't matter what it is as long as it feeds your fire.

EIGHT OF WANDS

NINE OF WANDS

NINE OF WANDS
Realm: The Desert and Volcanoes

Stretching creative thinking, seeing beyond physical limitations, intuitive understanding, knowing where your own skills end and others' begin

In the past…
your creative process was bogged down by overthinking. You relied so much on what you had learned that you failed to consider what else you may not know. To become more of an expert, you had to find where you could be a beginner again.

At present…
snakes, scorpions, and lizards work as individuals on a painting all at the same time. At first it is overwhelming and a bit chaotic to watch. Some sort of magick makes it all work and each artist shines within the cohesive piece.

On the horizon…
a flurry of activity animates a large sculpture garden. Artists work to update their creations, gardeners tend to the flowers and trees, the bird feeders are carefully cleaned, repaired, and filled. The whole place is a living monument to pursuit of artistic refinement.

From above…
the sun beats down on intricately folded fabric left outside. You open a piece of cloth and find that the fading has created a beautiful pattern, the product of intuitive arrangement combined with knowledge of the effects of the sun.

Deep within…
you have the ability to discern true intuition from fear or projection. This gift was not stumbled upon, it was developed as a skill through trial and error and hard work. Your inner world and outer vision are clear and true.

TEN OF WANDS
Realm: The Desert and Volcanoes

Performing at full power, creating a body of work, having nothing left to prove, effortless manifestation, collective consciousness in action

In the past…
you were very conscious of your own performance when working in a group. As you got more comfortable it became clear that you excelled beyond expectations when you focused on others, responding to their needs as if they were your own.

At present…
a troupe of dragons performs feats of acrobatic excellence. Their bodies all fit together as one to build a tall pyramid, their work so well practiced that it is now an effortless manifestation of who they are as a collective.

On the horizon…
performers on a flying trapeze soar high above the ground. Their languid grace of movement betrays none of the precision and exertion of their work. They don't even look before throwing themselves into the air, trusting their partners to catch them.

From above…
a chorus of voices sings in perfect time and harmony. The sound of their song reverberates through your body, bringing tears to your eyes and joy to your heart. You feel connected to them physically by the power of their sound waves.

Deep within…
your body, everything solid seems to fade into light and vapor. There is no longer any separation between you and the world. You are one and your actions reflect the care you have for the entire collective.

TEN OF WANDS

PAGE OF WANDS

PAGE OF WANDS
Realm: The Desert and Volcanoes

Experimentation, improvisation, creative play, wandering aimlessly, reinventing the wheel, trusting your gut, coloring outside the lines

In the past...
in a rush to finish painting your walls, you tripped and dropped a bucket of paint. As the pool of color spread, you dipped a toe in and pulled a bright stripe out, then another, then jumped in with both feet to create an energetic abstract mural on the floor.

At present...
you watch a young dragon practice juggling flaming wands, trying different moves and techniques, dropping and picking them back up again. You cannot see any signs of frustration, just an easy joy in the experience of learning.

On the horizon...
plumes of fireworks swirl in the sky dusted with brilliant sparks of gold and green. Images are formed and dissolved in the abstract field. You move your arms fluidly through the air as if conducting the explosions.

From above...
the chirping of crickets organizes into an orchestral arrangement. You try to recognize the tune, but it keeps changing and evolving. Soon you are dancing, creating your own improvised moves in time with the hypnotic sounds.

Deep within...
energy is bubbling up, making you feel restless and inspired. There is no time to think about what to do, you need to move and figure it out along the way, allowing new modes of creation to take form in your body.

KNIGHT OF WANDS
Realm: The Desert and Volcanoes

Passion, intense action, pursuit of goals, feeling it out, racing to the finish line, risk of exhaustion, difficulty with moderation

In the past…
you regularly burned the candle at both ends, oscillating between periods of intense creation and utter fatigue. Your passion and creativity needed the help of your intuition to guide your pace and your path. Then invigoration replaced your fatigue.

At present…
your muscles twitch and your heartbeat quickens. You can't tell if it's fear or excitement you feel. Though the knight and lizard are still, the air around them glows with energy as if they could spring to action at any moment.

On the horizon…
a light glows in the distant darkness. You focus on the flame and empty your mind, allowing your instinct to take over. An issue of great importance lies ahead and you must amp up your many powers to tackle it effectively.

From above…
lightning cracks across the sky. Two knights are engaged in battle, swooping through the air on the backs of dragons, their flaming swords send electric shocks through the clouds when they clash. You jump to your feet, ready to act.

Deep within…
a smoldering passion burns in your heart. You have kept it contained for a long time, but can't for much longer. Others are starting to see the smoke and soon you will be engulfed in the flame of your ardor.

KNIGHT OF WANDS

QUEEN OF WANDS

QUEEN OF WANDS
Realm: The Desert and Volcanoes

Empathy, expressing emotion through art, conjuring relationships, psychic soothing, allowing the heart to guide action, love magick

In the past…
you absorbed the emotions of everyone around you. You cherished your ability to empathize with others, but it became difficult to sort your own feelings from everyone else's. A little alone time let you cultivate the energetic boundaries you needed.

At present…
the Queen of Fire holds a magick wand out to you and you instinctively know the wand is now yours. This is an initiation. As you touch the wand, electricity shoots through your body, then settles to glow in your heart. You bow in gratitude.

On the horizon…
symbols appear written in fire on a hillside. They are not from any language you know or have even seen, yet you feel the message deeply. You have a directive from your heart and need to rest up before you begin.

From above…
the twinkling of fireflies lights up the night sky. You lie down on the ground to enjoy the show, resting your head on the soft grass. The glow of the insects pulses in a pattern that calms and opens your heart.

Deep within…
potent magick flows through your veins like lava, pumping through your heart to carry your desires out to your hands to be conjured and created. To maintain your power, you must keep it circulating in the world, inspiring those around you.

KING OF WANDS
Realm: The Desert and Volcanoes

Speaking through creative expression, planning out actions, decoding symbolic language, sensing the right thing to say, study of high magick

In the past...
you navigated the world intuitively without understanding why you were drawn to or repelled by specific things, places, or people. Stumbling upon a symbolic dictionary at a bookstore, you began to connect the dots.

At present...
the King of Fire commands your attention, directing your gaze with a flaming wand. Though no words are spoken between you, you understand the message you are given clearly. It is time to create what you have been dreaming of.

On the horizon...
a volcano erupts, shooting lava and ash high into the sky. You are startled by the sudden destruction, then fascinated by the new landscape being created before your very eyes. Your vision of a new world clarifies as you watch the lava flow and solidify.

From above...
sparks rain down around you, setting tiny fires that burn out within seconds. You hold your arm out and catch one in your hand. The spark catches fire and a tiny lavender flame burns, cupped in your palm, without causing you harm.

Deep within...
your mind, a flame flickers to life. The creative experimentation you've been engaged in has a direction and a purpose that is clear to you now. Your plan is set, the ability to will it into action burns inside you.

KING OF WANDS

ACKNOWLEDGMENTS

First and foremost, Rohan Daniel Eason, you are an absolute gift. I continue to be blown away, not only by your incredible artistic talent, but also by your uncanny ability to draw on paper what I have in my head (but much, much better) while remaining utterly pleasant under stress. I am so grateful for your collaboration and your friendship.

Big thanks to Jenny Dye for your editorial guidance, Sally Powell and Emily Breen, for your artistic vision and design, and to everyone at CICO, Penny Craig, Patricia Harrington, Leslie Harrington, and Kristine Pidkameny for believing in my vision.

Thank you my dear friends Dhani Harrison for your magick wands and Leigh Stone for your woodland portal.

Anne Woodward, you are stuck with me. I am never letting you and your incredible wisdom and humor go. Thank you for always being my voice of reason and my favorite dinner partner.

Chris, my love, my wizard, you make it all possible. Thank you.

And thank you to you—the witches and magicians and flame holders of the world, working for the good of all beings.

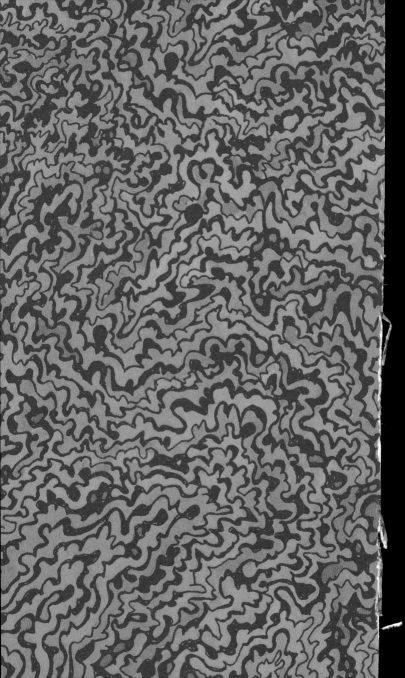